# Essays of Encouragement

## lynnmarie earl

ISBN:978-0-9835483-1-7

 Book/Cover Design & Typesetting by Michael Goodwin
mgoodwin@mgoodwin*DESIGN*.com
www.mgoodwin*DESIGN*.com

# Dedication

This book is dedicated first to our Lord and Savior, Jesus Christ. I truly believe the vast majority of what I share, both in speaking engagements and written material, are messages the Lord gives me, that I simply write down. To Him be the glory for I am nothing without Him.

Further, I do dedicate this book to my family – my sweet husband, Rick, who is supportive of this work. Our daughter, Asha Brooke, who has helped me with scores of computer questions; our son, Zane, who offers insight and thoughts about spiritual matters; and our son, Tucker, who is incredibly supportive and encouraging!

# Acknowledgements

There are always people who add to the success of a book, whether or not they realize it. First, we need to acknowledge the supporters of Realm Ministries. Without your prayer and financial support, this book, in fact this ministry, would not exist.

Second, we need to acknowledge our Board of Directors. This is a great group of people who take time out of their lives to support and give direction to this ministry and serve the Lord.

Third, the great churches and groups who invite me to speak and share the truth of the gospel. I value the relationships I have with each of you and look forward to continuing our relationships.

# Table of Contents

| | |
|---|---|
| Psalm 1 | 1 |
| Your Name in the Bible | 7 |
| Stop, Look, and Listen | 10 |
| If You Were A . . . | 16 |
| It's time for Lettuce | 20 |
| Don't Worry . . . Be Happy | 23 |
| Keep the Faith | 28 |
| David's To-Do List | 32 |
| Quiet Time | 37 |
| The Purpose of Storms | 40 |
| Create, An Attribute of God | 44 |
| The Prodigal Son | 49 |
| Stewardship | 55 |
| How Jesus Handled Bullies | 61 |
| When Life Gets Tough | 64 |
| Jesus is Light | 71 |
| You Can't Have the Good Without the Bad | 76 |
| Are you a Crier? | 80 |
| The Christian Life as a Piece of Furniture | 85 |
| How Old Are You? | 88 |
| Praying Hard Prayers | 91 |
| Meeting the Kids | 95 |
| Fall to be Lifted Up | 98 |
| Camping Out or Moving In? | 101 |

An Angel's Tale                                    105

Prayer Time                                        110

Forgiveness                                        114

What To Do When You
Don't Know What To Do                              118

LOL                                                123

You Are What You Eat                               127

Jesus was Born to . . .                            131

If . . . Then Promises                             135

Being Thankful for What We Have,
Not What We Want                                   140

Born to . . .                                      142

The Roman Road                                     144

Full Obedience                                     149

When We're Mistaught                               152

Accepting Gifts                                    159

# Psalm 1

Starting a new year means a whole bunch of new beginnings. New resolutions for some, new diets and exercise plans for many, new relationships for others. I'm taking a new approach to this month's article by dissecting a Psalm. I absolutely love the first Psalm, and while it's only six short verses, it is so full of imagery and meaning that it will take an entire article, and could take much longer. I'll do my best to be brief. You're welcome to get your Bible and follow along, but to make it easier, I'm copying the Psalm below.

[1] Blessed is the man who does not walk in the counsel of the wicked or stand in the way of sinners or sit in the seat of mockers.
[2] But his delight is in the law of the Lord, and on His law he meditates day and night.
[3] He is like a tree planted by streams of water which yields its fruit in season and whose leaf does not wither. Whatever he does prospers.
[4] Not so the wicked! They are like chaff that the wind blows away.
[5] Therefore the wicked will not stand in the judgment, nor sinners in the assembly of the righteous.

[6] For the Lord watches over the way of the righteous, but the way of the wicked will perish.

Let's start at the beginning. Before we get to the verses, it's helpful to understand that poetry, which is what Psalms are, in ancient Hebrew often used parallelism.[1] We see it often in the book of Proverbs, too:  Proverbs 15:1 – "A gentle answer turns away wrath, but a harsh word stirs up anger."  Proverbs 16:1 – "To man belongs the plans of the heart, but from the Lord comes the reply of the tongue."  Proverbs 17:1 – "Better a dry crust with peace and quiet than a house full of feasting, with strife."  Contrast made the writer's point very clear.

Second, it's helpful to know that there are five megathemes in the Psalms:  Praise, God's power, Forgiveness, Thankfulness, and Trust.[2] This first Psalm, as many in the first book of Psalms (Psalms 1 – 41), is a Psalm of Praise.  It was probably written by David, as many of the poems in this first book are.

Getting to the verses, we immediately see the word Blessed.  The word here means joyful and happy, specifically a happiness from God.  So, we're told we'll be blessed based on what we're about to be told.  That means we'll be joyful and have happiness from God if we . . . do not walk in the counsel of the wicked, stand in the way of sinners, or sit in the seat of mockers.

Let's think about this.  Do we really want to walk in the counsel of the wicked?  Do we want to stand in the way of sinners or sit with mockers?  Of course not.  I do my best, at my advanced age, to stay far away from sinners and mockers.  But it can be hard.  How many of us work with and even live with tempters and mockers?  How many of us ARE tempters and mockers?  When we

---

[1] The Quest Study Bible
[2] The Life Application Bible

offer dessert to a friend we know is watching their weight, or make a joke at someone's expense, just to be funny, we're the tempters and mockers.  Or we (I) invite somebody shopping who we know needs to watch their budget and use sarcasm to get a laugh, we're the tempters and mockers.  Please don't misunderstand me, dear saints.  I'm not throwing stones, because my house is made of very fragile glass.  I'm just aware that it's easy to slip into worldly habits because we are in, but not of, the world.  If we avoid being these people, and being around these people, the Lord can bring us joy and happiness.  This is a great beginning.  Let's look at verse two, my favorite of the six.

"But his delight is in the law of the Lord, and on His law he meditates day and night."

First note the difference of whether the pronouns are capitalized or not.  In King James Bibles, the translators capitalized pronouns when they referred to the Lord, Jesus, or the Holy Spirit.  I've done this in my own Bibles because it makes the Scripture so much clearer.  Our delight is in the law of the Lord, and we should be meditating on this day and night.

I've found the easiest way to meditate on Scripture is to memorize it.  That way, if I wake up in the middle of the night, I can meditate on His law and take delight in it.  This doesn't work for everyone, and I've found it's much harder to memorize with age, but what a delight when you know Scripture!  Meditation got such a bad reputation in the 1960's, so isn't it interesting to see that it's a Biblical concept?

Verse 3 says, "he (those who avoid trouble and meditate on the law of the Lord) is like a tree planted by streams of water, which yields its fruit in season and whose leaf does not wither.  Whatever he does prospers."

Wow!  Excuse me, but let me repeat myself.  Wow!  This is a wonderful promise from the Lord.  We will be like trees planted by streams of water.  Trees planted by streams get fed from underground (like all trees, I know), from a pretty consistent source of water. We're not cacti in the desert that have to hoard our water for the dry times. And, if that isn't enough, the word streams here means canals or rivers—as in flowing, unstoppable, running water. It's not a trickle, it just keeps coming. It keeps us alive and healthy. Remember, you can go longer without food than without water. And we have a river of it, waiting for us to dip in our toes, or leaves. We can bathe in rivers! Rivers can carry large boats full of cargo and people. Rivers can overrun a town when they overflow their banks. Rivers can power energy plants. The water in a river is very powerful, thus the swift current.

And the verse just gets better. We'll yield our fruit in season. Fruit in the Biblical sense is usually people, as in the number of people you've introduced or lead to Jesus. If you've ever felt fruitless, it's okay. God knows exactly when you'll produce a bountiful harvest. His timing is not ours, and His is perfect!

Finally, whatever we do will prosper. Now, we need to remember that this means what we're doing in the Lord's will. You can't use this verse to be a successful bank robber, but then, I know who's reading this, and that isn't a problem, dear readers. But what a wonderful promise that what we do will prosper. I can live on that promise for the rest of my life. It's the Lord's will that you have a happy and successful marriage; it's the Lord's will that you raise your children in the ways of the Lord. It's the Lord's will that you grow in your Christian life to be more like Jesus every day.

We have to continue, although I could camp on any of these three verses for days. How blessed am I to even read these verses, and the joy and happiness of the Lord are definitely with me as I write.

"Not so the wicked! They are like chaff that the wind blows away." That's verse four. Remember what was said above, in ancient Hebrew parallelism was used to make a point.  So now that we've seen how the righteous man is meditating on Scripture and being blessed abundantly, we see that the wicked are being compared to the useless husks that come off the wheat.

In the olden days, when wheat was harvested, the husks were often still attached.  Once on the threshing room floor, people would pick up the kernels with pitchforks and toss them into the air.  This was called winnowing. The husks were so light, that as they descended after the wheat, the wind could blow them away, as worthless and just getting in the way.  That's the wicked.  They are so worthless that they'll be blown away and forgotten.  Would you want to be compared to the useless husks of wheat, with nothing of value to add?  The wind alone is enough to blow it away.  Have you ever accidentally bitten into the outer shell of something?  Yuck.  The only thing you can do when that happens is to spit it out.  If you don't, please excuse the crassness here, it will find another way out of your system.  It's useless and offers no value whatsoever.

Verse five continues the thought:  "Therefore the wicked will not stand in the judgment, nor sinners in the assembly of the righteous."  Now, without getting into a huge eschatological discussion, this could be referring to references in the Book of Revelation, which wouldn't be written for hundreds of years.  The saved will face the Lord, but our sin has been paid in full; the unsaved will stand before the great white throne (Revelation 20), and their debt is still unpaid.  Ouch.

6 "For the Lord watches over the way of the righteous, but the way of the wicked will perish."  This is another great promise, but it's double edged, as seen in Hebrews 4:12.  We're also seeing the poet end the psalm with parallelism.  While the Lord is watching over the righteous (remember, the word righteous means one who turns toward God), the wicked are perishing, again repeated in John 3:16 – "For God so loved the world that He gave His only begotten Son, so that whoever believes

in Him will not perish but have everlasting life." So John 3:16 takes Psalms 1:6 a step further. While on earth the Lord watches over us, until He grants us everlasting life in heaven. What a great thought on which to start the new year!

So there's Psalm 1:1-6. The most important thing to take from this Psalm is that the wheat represents those who have accepted Jesus as their personal savior and have the promise of heaven; the chaff are those who haven't. I pray you are all wheat, and if you're unsure of your place in heaven, that you speak with someone immediately. As I said, there's so much more to be said on these few verses, and I do pray, friends, that you pick up your Bible on a daily basis this year. Remember, the man who meditates on His law is the valuable meat of the harvest, while the useless husk represents the wicked. Let's be the valuable part of the wheat to our friends and family this year.

(January 2009)

# Your Name in the Bible

Have you ever looked for your name in the Bible?
It's in there.  It's actually in there repeatedly, but you
may not recognize it at first.  Before we look at where
your name is, let's look at where your name isn't.

In Exodus 3:14, the Scripture reads, "I am."  This
is the translation of the word Yahweh.  What God is
saying here is that He is God, which means, you are not.
I know we all know people with demi-god personalities.
Our culture actually creates a lot of these.
Entertainment idols, certain professions—did anyone's
mom ever pray that their daughter would marry a
carpenter?  I mean, it's a good profession, even good
enough for our Savior.  But moms want their daughters
to marry doctors.  And in our society, doctors earn
respect and money simultaneously.  I'm not taking away
from what these people have achieved, I'm pointing out
that our culture puts some of them on pedestals, and we
shouldn't be surprised when they act like they know
they're up there.

So where is your name in Scripture?  The place
you'll find it repeatedly is 1 Corinthians 13: 4–7.  In the
NIV, it reads: "Love is patient, love is kind.  It does not
envy, it does not boast. It is not proud.  It is not rude, it

is not self-seeking, it is not easily angered, it keeps no record of wrongs. Love does not delight in evil but rejoices with the truth. It always protects, always trusts, always hopes, always perseveres."

So, can you find your name? You may have heard this before, so you know the trick. Everyplace you see the word love, or the pronoun it, in place of love, you substitute your name. So Pat would read, "Pat is patient, Pat is kind. Pat does not envy, Pat does not boast. Pat is not proud. Pat is not rude, Pat is not self-seeking, Pat is not easily angered, Pat keeps no record of wrongs. Pat does not delight in evil but rejoices with the truth. Pat always protects, always trusts, always hopes, always perseveres."

Now, it's one thing to read it when you're in a good, quiet mood reading this. The question is living it. Are you patient, kind, not envious or boastful? It's a lot to ask! But remember, God is love, and through His Son, Jesus Christ, we are becoming more like Christ on a daily basis. Some days are harder than others. We know that. The prayer is that when you find your name in the Bible, you can remember to make an attempt to live up to it.

Another place you'll find your name is John 3:16. This is such a famous verse, thanks to all the sports fans who bring their signs to games. You may read it as, "For God so loved the world that He gave His only begotten Son, so that whoever believes in Him may not perish, but have everlasting life." But, when you (or we'll use Jane) are (is) looking for your name, it would read, "For God so loved Jane, that He gave His only begotten Son, so that Jane, by believing in Him, may not perish, but have everlasting life." Isn't that a great promise? And it's personal. It's a promise from our Lord to us individually.

Let's look at just two verses from the gospel of John. John 14:21 reads, "Whomever has My commands and obeys them, he is the one who loves Me." John 14:23 says, "If anyone loves Me, he will obey My teaching. My Father will love him, and We will come to him and make our home with him." These verses have me beside myself with excitement. Let's rewrite them, using our own names. Whenever you see the word whomever in the Bible, any Christian can definitely use their name there. So these verses taken together, for Chris, will read, "Chris has My commands and obeys them. Chris is the one who loves Me. If Chris loves Me, Chris will obey My teaching. My Father will love Chris, and We will come to Chris and make our home with Chris." Don't you want to be Chris? The Father and Jesus will come and make their home with us. How can it get any better? Isn't it great to find your name in there? The Bible wasn't just written to some ancient people; it's living and active (Hebrews 4:12) and is all about you!

Your name is all over that Bible, but you need to read it in a whole new way. Today or tomorrow, whatever you're reading in the Bible, see if you can find your name among the pages. Some are easier to find than others (Psalm 139:14 – "for I am fearfully and wonderfully made" becomes "for (your name here) is fearfully and wonderfully made." Other instances may be harder to find, but you're in there. The Lord loves you and wrote you a very long love letter telling you how much. Enjoy reading it on a personal level.
(October 2007)

# Stop, Look, and Listen

This month's article very much wrote itself on Wednesday, May 13th, when I was climbing Ochos Rios in Jamaica, mon. While many of you already know about Jamaica's number one tourist attraction, please allow me to briefly explain to the readers who, like myself, are new to this international tourist site.

Once you arrive at Dunns River Park, you walk down a trail next to this lovely, not-steep waterfall. The rocks have had thousands of years to be eroded by water to have no sharp edges left. At the bottom, you leave the trail and get in the very cold water. We were put in groups of about a dozen, and the first thing you do in the water is hold hands with your neighbor, whether or not you know them.

Holding hands is necessary for a few reasons. One, it's a good team-building moment. It's normal to exchange at least first names with someone who's holding your hand. But, the 900 foot ascent you're about to take has two additional things that require hand-holding. One is a current that can be strong enough to knock you off your feet, and if someone isn't holding you, you can bump yourself hard on those nicely eroded very large rocks. Second, there are several places on the walk that the next step is so unnatural and awkward that it takes someone pulling (and/or pushing) you to allow you to advance.

Now, here alone is probably enough material for a plethora of articles on the importance of relying on others. As this is a Christian article, our reliance would be on the Lord. There is nothing you can do in this world all alone. Not to bring up a negative subject in the midst of a beautiful waterfall, but when you hear sad stories about teenagers who make very bad decisions, rarely are they the ones with friends calling them all hours of the day and night. We all need others.

By the way, being in Jamaica with a group of people from my husband's office, I decided to play the part of a hostess and often approached people who were standing alone at different functions. I would ask a question or two, and these people were off and running. Everyone there, and these were successful employees who had won this trip, were all eager, even hungry, for attention. Try it sometime. See how long it takes to engage another person in talking about themselves.

Back to the falls. It soon became evident that the best way to avoid falling in the frigid water was to keep your eye on the water and your next step. This brings to mind Psalm 119:105 – "Your word is a lamp unto my feet and a light unto my path." If you weren't paying attention directly in front of and behind you, you could easily make a misstep. While in this case the misstep would probably only dunk you, I think we can all appreciate the broader implications of missteps in our lives. There are some bad decisions I've made in my past that I wish only resulted in a cold dunking. Interestingly, it's probably easier to spot missteps in the lives of others, such as spouses, siblings, or children, but we are all subject to them. Again, there's more to say, but I think readers of this newsletter are mature enough to understand the implications.

At first, as you begin the walk, you're just concentrating on not falling. You're very concerned about those behind you, because it's your responsibility to pull them up. This has great Christian implications. It's not just our job as Christians to introduce unbelievers to Christ, but to help them on their own journey. Isn't it exciting to see others grow in their relationship with the Savior? In order to help others grow, you need to be one step ahead of them, so they should be encouraging your own study and growth.

Every now and then, in the falls, you come to a pool. These pools are about four feet deep. In the Christian analogy, the water could represent the Holy Spirit, grace and mercy, or just refreshment. Some people struggled through these pools, sad to be beyond their knees in the cold water. Others immersed themselves fully, enjoying the coolness. Some people chose to play in the water, splashing and being splashed. If you can close your eyes for a minute and relax your mind, imagine yourself in just such a pool, and your own response. Are you going to cautiously wade through, or are you going to jump in and immerse yourself in it? Are you going to grumble about the cold water being deeper than you realized, or will you accept it with a smile and keep going? As a Christian, are you jumping into the Christian walk, and immersing yourself in Christian fellowship and friends, or just wading through the absolute minimum?

Something as yet unsaid about these pools is that these are the only places where tiny pebbles reside. It's impossible to pass through a pool, because they're too shallow to swim, without having your required footwear fill with these pebbles. You can imagine the discomfort. Some, like myself, felt the need to sit and remove the small stones at the earliest possible moment. Others chose to walk with them, figuring more would come at each pool, which they did, and they waited until the end to dump all the pebbles at once. There have to be some great analogies in there about who chooses which option and why, but this article is long enough.

At this point we were about a third of the way up the 900 foot trip, so we'd traveled about the length of a football field.  Now, incredibly talented runners can travel that distance in less than a minute.  We'd been at it for 20 times that.  By now people were starting to feel more comfortable and hands were being dropped.  I was finally able to take my eyes off my feet and look around—and down.  Wow, what a view—Beautiful foliage and running water, tickling my ears, toes, and eyes.  What a splendid example of God's artistry.  I think I actually gasped at the beauty, even as I thought to myself, I almost missed this for looking at my toes.

How often does this happen to us?  How often are we so caught up with our to-do list and the demands on our lives that we don't look up and see the wonder that is our world?  Please, take time today and watch something—your child getting off the bus, people at a mall, a single flower growing, an old couple who still hold hands—stop and look and appreciate your world.  If I hadn't looked up from my climb, I would have missed a beautiful view.  I didn't have a camera with me, because mine isn't water proof and this is a very wet walk, but in some ways, that's better, because a photograph probably couldn't do justice to the memory picture I took at that moment.

So we continued the climb.  I saw people fall, but in every case they bounced back up, assuring everyone they weren't hurt, just very wet.  I watched the guides run up those falls.  Now, this is a lesson for us!  While it was the first trip for most of us up Dunns River Falls (we did have one return sojourner), the guides are there daily.  They helped when people needed a hand, they splashed if they thought someone wasn't having fun, they called to us and took pictures and videos of each group (to sell to us after).  We learned our guide's voice very quickly, which makes me think now of John 10:4 –

"and His sheep follow Him because they know His voice."
It didn't take us long to learn our guide's voice, and we
immediately trusted him. He was there to help us, and
to make sure we were enjoying ourselves. What a
blessing! What a thought. Who in your life do you
encourage and help to enjoy themselves?

And watching those guides jump from rock to
rock, while we plodded slowly and carefully, is another
lesson. These guides were comfortable in the water
because they spend so much time there. How
comfortable are we in Scripture and in our daily walk?
How comfortable are we sharing the good news, and how
much more comfortable will we be when we spend more
time? I love the idea of splashing through Scripture,
running from verse to verse, knowing what's on the next
page before turning there.

Jesus loves you like no other in this world. He's
watching out for you, and the Holy Spirit was sent to be
your guide, and they want you to enjoy your life because
they do love you. In Matthew 7 Jesus asks which of us
would give our children a stone if they asked for bread.
That's a crazy thought. We want the best for our babies.
Dear saints, you are Christ's baby.

So the walk continued, right under the interstate.
We actually had to bend down to get past this manmade
necessity. It was an inconvenience, quite honestly.
Several people hit their head on the structure. But, the
entire time, nobody felt danger from the cars racing over
our heads. And I don't think anybody ever felt danger of
the river, although it was a powerful force. Why would
our daily life be any different? If God is taking care of us
on our play days, we have to know He's there on our
work days.

At the top, we all gathered to take a picture of our
accomplishment. We were able to look past the steps
that led out of the water, to see that the river continues,
but for now, this trip was at an end. Yes, there was
further to go, but not today, and not with this group. We

gathered, took our picture, and put our feet back on solid ground.  I still felt like I was walking on water for a few minutes, kind of like you do when you get off a boat or roller skates.  It had been a wonderful experience, but I wouldn't realize until I fell asleep at 8:45 that night how exhausting it had been.  I was tired!  But it was a good tired.  The kind of tired that comes from a job well done.

I learned some great things on that mountaintop experience.  First, to keep my eye on where I was going.  A misstep could have landed me in cold water.  Second, I'm dependent on others, especially my Lord and Savior.  Third, I have to stop and enjoy the journey, even as I continue my travels.  Fourth, challenges come:  the road built over the river was a challenge, some slick stones offered a challenge, and some little pebbles that got into our shoes was my biggest challenge.  Fifth, my being there affected other people.  Without me the groups may have been split differently.  I was near one of the few children on the trip, and I think she really liked having a female near her.  Somebody else would have been there for her, but it would have been a different dynamic.  Sixth, the trip isn't over for me until I breathe my last.  The road continues with or without you on it.

I pray you use every opportunity to praise the Lord and appreciate your surroundings, and don't wait for a trip to Jamaica or some other land to do it.  Blessings and miracles are all around you.  Please, right now, stop and look.

(June 2009)

# If You Were A . . .

We all have ways of describing ourselves, and most of them tend to be common and understood— spouses, parents, children, siblings, employees, volunteers. When you use these terms, people generally understand your meaning. There can be confusion, but we're communicating.

Then we're asked every now and then to describe ourselves with adjectives: outgoing, shy, talkative, tall, extrovert/introvert. The people who are willing to get past the physical attributes are truly revealing more about themselves.

Have you ever been asked to describe yourself as a noun? You know, if you were a tree/flower/house, etc. These are fun games, especially when played with people who know us well. Let's take a word from Scripture and see how well it fits you. If you were a vessel, what type of vessel would you be?

What do you even think about when the word vessel is used, because it really isn't much of a 21$^{st}$ century word. I'll pull up dictionary.com and see what it says: 1. A craft for traveling on water—not where my mind went! 2. An airship—even further from where my mind went! 3. A hollow or concave utensil, as a cup, bowl, pitcher, or vase, used for holding liquids or other contents. Yep, this is what I had in mind. But that definition defines hundreds of items.

For instance, you might be a tea kettle, capable of providing warmth, and letting out a scream when it's ready to be used. It's a very serviceable vessel. What about a garden bucket? It can hold much more water than a tea kettle, but it can get too heavy to be toted around. It's also used for larger purposes than filling a small cup for tea or coffee. The bucket is going to be used to help wash the car or water plants—larger jobs. What about a spoon? Do you remember the game where you had to transport a cup of water, using nothing other than a spoon? While a spoon isn't the first thing you would consider as a vessel, it gets the job done, just very slowly. Think of some of your favorite pottery. It can be beautiful and intricate, and still used to hold liquids or other contents, even if you only use it as a decoration.

In the Bible, the word vessel is used hundreds of times, to carry anything from something as simple and necessary as water to something as extravagant and expensive as choice perfumes.

The point of any vessel, per the definition, is that it's hollow, so that it can be used to carry liquids or some other contents. When we come to our Lord to give our lives to Him, and accept Jesus as our Savior, it's our job to empty ourselves of all worldly sins, lusts, and wants. We want to empty ourselves so that we can be refilled with love, kindness, gentleness, and all the other fruit of the Spirit (see Galatians 5:22-23).

In 2 Tim 2:20-21, it says, "In a large house there are articles not only of gold and silver, but of wood and clay; some are for noble purposes and some for ignoble. If a man cleanses himself from the latter, he will be an instrument for noble purposes, made holy, useful to the Master and prepared to do any good work."

Now, which of these, given your druthers, would you like to be: gold, silver, wood, or clay? Don't assume everyone will have the same answer. I know some earthy people who are saying, "of course wood and clay. That's close to nature. That's close to God." While others are saying, "Nothing but the best. Gold all the way." There's no right answer. Whether you're gold or clay, the more important question is, are you being filled with things that will glorify the Lord so you can be used for noble purposes?

This isn't a beat-you-up session. It's intended to be encouraging, to see yourself in a new way. Look at yourself as an empty vessel. Are you going to fill this beautiful vessel—we're all beautiful in God's sight, so don't argue with me here—with profound thoughts, kind words, Scripture memorization, compassion, love, and generosity? If you do, the Lord will be able to use you mightily.

Think how many people you touch in a day. Even the stay-home moms and dads still come in contact with mail deliverers, store clerks, neighbors, and sales reps, if only by phone. Take time daily to think about your vessel, and fill it every morning with fresh thoughts of love, joy, peace, patience, kindness, goodness, faithfulness, gentleness, and self-control (we're back to the fruit of the Spirit). In that way you will be useful to the Master—can you think of a greater joy?

2 Timothy continues to say, "and prepared to do any good work." Are you prepared for any good work? For years and years I wanted to bring people to Christ. I wanted to sit down and speak with them and show them in the Bible where it tells us how to be saved. Alas, that wasn't God's call for me at that time. I was a planter. Yep, a work in the dirt, get sweaty and hot, unfashionable in overalls, downright scruffy sower. This isn't glamorous! I couldn't walk into meetings and say, "Sorry I'm late. I was meeting with some people and lead all of them to Christ." That's what I wanted. Ah, notice the word I. It isn't what our Lord wanted at that time.

In truth, I wasn't prepared to do that good work. I was prepared to share my faith so openly by saying, "Praise the Lord, I had the funniest thing happen to me," or "The Lord is so kind, that . . . ." Those words get people's attention, and they're words that sow, but they are not words that reap in and of themselves.

I came to Christ alone in a Church. At that point I'd heard the gospel in various ways, but nobody took me by the hand, or for a walk, or opened a Bible. I found the Lord in His perfect timing, not mine. Without the experience of being led to the Lord the way I wanted to lead others, it was much more difficult for me to lead others to Christ—or so I thought.

So I realized, through Bible study, fellowship, Scripture memorization, and daily life, that I need to be prepared for any good work. That when I received a phone call saying, "The Smith's had their baby and need supper," that was my call to do a good work. And when the announcement came in Sunday School, "We're having a painting party for a young widow," that was my call to do a good work. Neither of these is glamorous, but for this I am prepared. I don't cook well, but I can put a meal together. And physical labor, PTL, is something I'm still capable of even as I near – uh uh, not saying my age.

I will never sing in a choir, because that's not the good work to which I'm called. I can type. I can type quickly. I can put thoughts on paper. If I fill my brain with nothing but sugar and sweetness, I won't have any good meat to offer. I try to give myself a diet of protein, carbs, and sweets, so that I can offer useful words, but temper them with sweetness.

As an empty vessel, I pray you will choose to be filled with the Holy Spirit, who has started a good work in you, and will see it through to completion. Fill your vessel and find your good work, so you will be useful to the Master.

(August 2009)

# It's time for Lettuce

With summer coming, now is the perfect time to add some lettuce to our diet.  No, I'm not talking about eating here, although that is one of my favorite topics, especially if it involves chocolate. I'm well aware that diet is a four-letter word, but it can change from a negative to a positive when approached correctly.  I mean, love is a four-letter word, too.

Let's talk about lettuce in terms of **Let Us**.  In chapter 10 of Hebrews, from verses 19-25, we are given five Let us to do's, something for us to chew on.  They are, paraphrased:  Let us draw near; let us hold unswervingly; let us consider how we may spur one another to love and good deeds; let us not give up meeting together; and let us encourage one another.

Now, if we added these five pieces of lettuce to our diets, all at once, or one a day, or whatever works for you, how would our lives, and those of our families, be changed in a month?  Six months?  A year?

Let's start with the first.  Let us draw near.  That sounds great! We all want to be near to the Lord. Imagine a strange- looking ladder, with not two sides, but several. This ladder has exactly enough sides for everyone in your family.  Now, if God is at the top of that ladder, and you're drawing near to Him, and your spouse is on another side of that ladder, drawing nearer to the Lord, what's happening between you?  You're drawing nearer to each other.  And your children, or parents, or siblings, are on the other rungs on other sides of this demented-shaped ladder.  As you all approach the Lord, you also grow nearer to each other, which puts you all in a great place—closer together, and closer to God!

Bite two of our lettuce:  Let us hold unswervingly.  Now, in Hebrews, the unknown writer (which is a whole other discussion), is saying to hold onto the hope we profess, for He who promised is faithful.  I think we can stay on that same ladder here.  Have you ever seen a rickety ladder, one that didn't look like it would hold you at all? But, you have to climb it.  You can think literally or figuratively here.  We've all been on what looked like an unstable ladder before.  Well, we don't have to HOPE the ladder is safe, we KNOW it is, because the Lord who made that ladder is FAITHFUL.  So go on and climb, with confidence.

Next, our bite is spurring one another to love and good deeds.  Well, would you rather be the person wearing the spurs, or the horse being spurred?  They're both good and bad places to be.  It's good to be carried, but it's good to carry others.  We rest when we're on top, but we grow stronger from holding the weight.  The point is, on a daily basis, spur one another on to love and good deeds.  Call that friend, encourage your sister, write that card.  As you spur others, you'll find yourself being drawn to love and good deeds, too.

I hope you're not too full for the next bite, because it's a mouthful:  let us not give up meeting together.  I think we're looking for more than Sunday mornings here.   Let's make every meeting a time of rejoicing and glory to our Lord.  The next time you say good morning at work, MEAN IT.  Wish people a GOOD morning.  Find a Bible study, or create your own.  Go to church, and stay for Sunday school.  Call and invite friends over for a time of food, fun, and fellowship on a Friday night. Okay, too many F's there, but alliteration can be fun.

Our final piece of lettuce:  let us encourage one another. You want to know what I think the best part of this one is? It costs us very little—really, nothing. Encourage one another—pat someone on the back; compliment a dress or suit; notice a new pair of glasses. Just smile and say, "It's so nice to see you." That's encouragement. That makes people want to keep doing what they're doing.

Don't bite off more than you can chew, but adding some lettuce to your diet can prove to make you a more beautiful person.

(April 2007)

# Don't Worry ... Be Happy

Oh, July. We're in the thick of summer now. And your weather may feel thick. As this is our first summer in Georgia, I'm being reminded what humidity really feels like. I admit I love it, but I'm feeling it.

But, it's summer, so we're supposed to be having a great time. Life is good. The living is easy, as a very old song goes. You don't have to admit if you remember the song, because it would tell your age.

So, it's a great idea to not worry and be happy, but how to do it? It's almost like Mark Twain's line, "Everybody complains about the weather, but nobody does anything about it." Everybody says to not worry and be happy, but how? Well, I found lots of how-to's right in the Bible, and we'll discuss several of them. Some I'm saving for another newsletter, because there is just so much in the Bible. What a blessing in itself!

First let's look at Psalm 46:10 – "Be still and know that I am God." I'm not even using any specific translation, because this verse is so well known. But, as well as I know it, how often do I follow it? Every time I find myself stressed or anxious (angst is one of my favorite words), I find that I'm missing Psalm 46:10 in my life. So I get still and listen and talk to the Lord.

Second, let's look at Romans 16:17 from the NIV (which correlates well with 2 John 10, for those who love cross referencing): "I urge you, brothers, to watch out for those who cause divisions and put obstacles in your way that are contrary to the teaching you have learned. Keep away from them." Now, I'm guessing there are people in your life who don't leave you feeling good after a chat. This Scripture advises us to stay away from them. There, permission, right from the Bible. You are taught to watch out for people who cause trouble. This doesn't mean disrespect them, and certainly don't gossip about them, but to keep your distance. The last sentence of this verse, *Keep away from them* in the NIV, is very strong when stated in the original Greek. Take this direction seriously, and you can worry less and be happier.

I remember, years ago, I had a friend I had lunch with regularly. I learned a lot from our conversations, and gained wisdom through her. One of my challenges at that time was a person in my life who was very negative. Being on the outside, my friend could very objectively and without judging see this person's effect on me. And she simply told me at lunch one day that I needed to avoid this person. Oh, my gosh. What an idea. Remove the negative influence, the negative feedback I always got, the questions about any decision I made—how obvious! I took her advice and reduced time with this person greatly. The woman is still in my life, but as I've grown as a person and a Christian, she doesn't wield the influence on me that she once did, so I can be around her without coming away feeling horrible. Even though I was saved at the time, I didn't realize my friend was giving me Biblical advice, and I'm sure she didn't either. The best advice can so often be traced back to Scripture.

In Romans 12:10 we are told to "Be devoted to one another in brotherly love. Honor one another above yourselves." The first question is whether this verse contradicts the one above.  Definitely, surely, unequivocally, NOT.  The above verse was about choosing to not spend time with negative influences.  This verse tells us to be devoted to other people.  If the person you are choosing to not spend time with above calls you for help, then treat them with love and help them.  But this doesn't mean you have to celebrate with them afterwards.  Get the job done and go, because if the negativity is real, it will return.

Roman 12:10 tells us (as does Phil 2:3, again for cross referencers) to honor others.  You can honor others by being a good listener, by anticipating needs, by sending a card, and in a host of other ways.  The point here is that if you are concentrating on others, and truly honoring your spouse, children, family, co-workers, and neighbors, not to mention clerks and other drivers on the road, then your life will be happier and less stressful.

Next let's look at Ephesians 4:2 – "Be completely humble and gentle; be patient, bearing with one another in love."  This verse completes both of the verses above, showing how well the Bible works together.  If you are truly humble (and we know the Lord blesses the humble), then you will be honoring others above yourself.  Think about it—that's what humility is. Patience is one of the fruit (not fruits) of the Spirit (Galatians 5:22), so you're honoring the Trinity as well, in obedience.  When you choose ahead of time to get along with others, and you choose to be humble and gentle in all interaction, you will truly have a less divisive, happier lifestyle.  Will you have to give up some things you want?  Possibly.  But don't those things pale in comparison with what you'll get for eternity?  I'm not asking you to be a doormat here, just consider how important some decisions really are.  I truly believe that you'll find, as you sow humility and gentleness, you'll reap an amazing harvest of the same. That will definitely lead to a happier life.

2 Timothy 2:23 is probably my favorite NIV verse in the entire Bible. I can still remember where I was the first time I read it—packing for a family reunion. When you read the verse here, you'll appreciate how timely the Lord's word is: "Don't have anything to do with foolish and stupid arguments, because you know they produce quarrels." Now, the verses that surround this are also great ideas of what to do on a daily basis, but this verse alone has gotten me through some tough times.

Some people like to fight. They enjoy verbal sparring, and they probably know what buttons to push to get you going. But, those oral fisticuffs leave everyone feeling frustrated, possibly angry, and definitely not happy. Here, the Bible is telling us to have nothing to do with these arguments (not the people, just the arguments). I know it's hard to keep your mouth closed when antagonizing remarks are made, but the Bible answers that question with James 1:19—"Everyone should be quick to listen, slow to speak, and slow to become angry." There's your advice, from both sides. HAVE NOTHING TO DO WITH FOOLISH AND STUPID ARGUMENTS. What a concept. Don't we already know this? Yet, we get suckered into the discussions, which does not bode well for the theory of not worrying and being happy. If you do get stuck in such a discussion, then BE SLOW TO SPEAK AND SLOW TO BECOME ANGRY.

If we return to our direction to be humble and patient, we can get around, out of, or away from these arguments. That will lead to less worry and more happiness. From personal experience I can say, it really does feel great. Sadly, I have more experience from the other side, of letting myself be coerced into the foolish and stupid arguments. And then I spend time kicking myself for getting dragged into them—this is a much better way, I can attest from experience. By the way, that family gathering went much better as I practiced this verse that entire weekend. Not one fight.

So, in conclusion, Scripture tells us to avoid the negative, concentrate on others, and do the right thing. Yes, you're thinking, but it's one thing to sit here and read the verses and agree with them, it's another to actually live this way, especially if not everyone in your circle ascribes to Christian beliefs.  But you, dear saints, have the secret.  How do you succeed in incorporating these Scriptures into your lives?  With one more verse:

Hebrews 12:2-3 says:  "Let us fix our eyes on Jesus, the author and perfecter of our faith, Who, for the joy set before Him, endured the cross, scorning its shame, and sat down at the right hand of the throne of God.  Consider Him who endured such opposition from sinful men, so that you will not grow weary and lose heart."  Let's concentrate on fixing our eyes on our Lord, Jesus, and we'll be more than half way home.  You can trust Jesus to meet you there.

(July 2007)

# Keep the Faith

I hope you're having a great day and had a great month of January. Ours turned colder than I thought was allowed in Georgia, but as it was our first January in the state, I don't have anything to compare. But, statistically, by now people's excitement over their new beginning is beginning to wan. Resolutions have been broken and are left behind, forgotten. Well, if the resolution was of material or earthly consequence, it's not a great loss in terms of eternity. While the extra pounds may seem like a big deal now, they mean NOTHING in heaven. Nothing.

But let's look toward the mountains, where our help comes from (Psalm 121:1). Scripture kindly offers us many verses of how to keep faith, through dark winter days, and hot summer days; through challenges with children and with bosses; through insufficient funds and less than enough time. Let's see what the Good Book tells us today.

As some have learned, Hebrews Chapter 11 is called the Great Faith Chapter of the Bible. That was a lot of capital letters! Here we find the Hall of Fame of great believers. I'd love to have my name added to that list. While we won't see it on this list, we can be sure our name is on the list for heaven. Our name is written in the book of life when we accept Jesus as our Savior. But beyond that, we're called to be faithful, and to keep the faith, as our predecessors.

Hebrews 11:1 says, in the NIV, "Now faith is being sure of what we hope for, and certain of what we do not see." The word certain here translates as evidence or conviction. Are you truly convicted of what you can't see? I am so tired of conversations with unbelievers who complain that Christianity all comes down to faith. Of course it does! But then, so do lots of things. I don't do the math every time I sit on a new chair. I just trust that it will hold my weight. And as for evolution, I truly don't have enough faith to believe that a monkey turned into a man, or that a dolphin came ashore and turned into a cow. My faith isn't based on that. My faith is in the Lord, the Maker of Heaven and Earth.

Let's jump to the Old Testament for a minute. If you like your own translation, or want to make notes in your Bible, by all means, feel free to use your own Bible. But for the convenience of readers, I'll tell you that Psalm 46:10 says, "Be still, and know that I am God; I will be exalted among the nations, I will be exalted in the earth."

This isn't just rhetoric. It's a promise! But, there is a caveat. The original Hebrew word for our word still tells us to stop struggling and fighting. So, we do have the responsibility of being still. Then, we will know that Yahweh is God. The rest of the verse refers to Jesus' millennial reign. Jesus will return, and while I pray it's in my lifetime, I'm not sure the world is bad enough yet to cause Him to return so soon. Some writers of New Testament letters expected Jesus to return, literally, any minute. I pray He comes soon, and when He does, He will reign for a thousand years, and this prophesy will be fulfilled. In the meantime, our job is to know that He is God. There's your faith!

Let's return to the New Testament and look up Galatians 6:9. I love this verse and find myself quoting it to myself and my children often. It says, "Let us not become weary in doing good, for at the proper time we will reap a harvest if we do not give up." There are several to-do's in this verse. First, we need to not become weary. No worries there, because Philippians 4 tells us we can survive on the Lord's strength, and back in Psalm 40 we were told we can soar as eagles. This part is covered for us!

Then we're told, in God's timing, and His timing is always perfect, even if we don't understand it, we WILL reap a harvest. We will! The harvest is ours. But, if we have any farmers out there, they'll tell us that reaping a harvest is hard work. And, you can't give up. You can't pick half the harvest and come back later for the rest, because it won't be there. Weeds will strangle the plants, birds will steal the fruit of the harvest. So, we have some things to do. First, keep doing good things, and don't get tired of it, even if it doesn't seem like you're making a dent. Second, don't give up while we look forward to that harvest. I'm not sure what kind of feasts there are in heaven, but I'm sure they're something we've never experienced on earth. And is there anything better than chocolate? There could be, and if so, heaven has it—that's my harvest.

Finally, just as a reminder that we're not alone in our faith walk, let's return to Hebrews, but this time Hebrews 12:3 – "Consider Him who endured such opposition from sinful men, so that you will not grow weary and lose heart."

Again we're talking about weariness, but this time it's a promise, not a warning. How cool is this? In our faith, when we consider Jesus, Who went through so much more, undeservedly, than any of us, we will not grow weary and lose heart. I can do that! Something I can get my head and heart around. The next time the kids are screaming, or the boss is demanding, or the

woman across the hall at work is sneering, or the check isn't coming, I can consider Jesus, and I will not grow weary and lose heart.  What a concept!  I love the blessings God has for me, and I just need to take hold of them, and enjoy them as they pour on my head.
(February 2008)

# David's To-Do List

David, in 1 Chronicles 16:7-37, offers the Lord a beautiful Psalm of Thanks. In this song, in verses 8-12, we are given several to-do's. Now, I know life is busy for everyone, but no matter what you have on your list for today, or how busy you are, everyone has enough time to give thanks to the Lord. Even if you praise Him while showering or cooking or driving, you can find time to give thanks. David's song ends reiterating that we should give thanks and praise, but let's look specifically at the first few verses, and what David told us to do so many years and generations ago.

First, in verse 8, we're told to Give Thanks to the Lord. That sounds easy, right? In truth, if we spent even ten straight minutes actually enumerating our blessings, we wouldn't be close to finished. In fact, often when I'm giving thanks in prayer, I get distracted, so I don't know if I could give thanks for ten straight minutes without interruption. I have made lists of thanks, and the pages run into one another. I'm talking about specific thanks here, not just the general.

For instance, thank the Lord for the health of each and every family member. Again, not a general, thank you we're healthy. But, when you hear about the diseases and challenges people face daily, thank the Lord that your family is not so challenged (with apologies to those families facing these challenges). I even include thanks for my car when it's feeling well. I certainly offer prayers when it's in the shop, right?

Don't limit your thanksgiving to once a day. Use any moment, good or bad, to give thanks, as we're taught in 1 Thessalonians 5:18 – "give thanks in all circumstances, for this is God's will for you in Christ Jesus." So what David tells us to do in this prayer, Paul reiterates in a letter, hundreds of years later. I love consistency in Scripture! While you're driving, doing dishes, balancing a checkbook—stop and give thanks for your car, your food, and your income, among other things.

Verse 9 continues our list of to do's: "Sing to Him, sing praise to Him; tell of all His wonderful acts." Now, anybody who has read much of what I've written already knows I have no musical ability. Zero. Zilch. Nada. Even my youngest, as a baby, would put his hand over my mouth and say, "No sing, mommy." This child knew early that his mama can't sing. But, the Bible tells us repeatedly to make a joyful noise unto the Lord (Psalms 66, 81, 95, 98, and 100), and here it is again in 1 Chronicles. Sing to the Lord, Saints! Sing praises to Him. Call our Lord by name—Yahweh, El Shaddai, Mighty Counselor, Holy One; or call Him by attribute – Blesser, Redeemer, Merciful, Savior, Kindness, Gentleness—these are all attributes of our mighty Father. Calling Him by these attributes is a wonderful way to praise the Lord.

Don't you love hearing stories? I don't think any human, however old, gets tired of hearing a good story. And do you know what makes a story great? One about us. Don't your children love to hear stories about when they were young? Don't your parents love to hear stories you remember from your childhood? We love being the main characters in stories. And we're made in our Creator's (another good description with which to sing the Lord's praises) image, so our Father must like to hear stories about Himself, too. Then obey David's lesson and tell the Lord of His wonderful acts. Yes, He already knows them. Yes, He loves to hear you tell the story.

Verse ten has two great components: "Glory in His Holy name; let the hearts of those who seek the Lord rejoice." First, we're told to glory in God's holy name. We already know that holy means set apart. When we look up the word glory in a Bible dictionary, we hit gold! First, honor. Glorifying God means honoring Him—with our words, our thoughts, and our deeds.

Second, glory means "the glorious moral attributes, the infinite perfections of God[1]." That pretty much says it all right there. The infinite perfections of God means we can never finish glorifying Him, because His perfections are beyond time; beyond our understanding, in truth.

Third, and I like this one best, the phrase "Give glory to God," is a Hebrew idiom meaning, "Confess your sins."[2] Confessing our sins gives God glory—I just love the thought of that! Humility is a wondrous blessing.

But we're not done with verse ten yet. It continues, "let the hearts of those who seek the Lord rejoice." We get to rejoice! Isn't it perfectly logical that first we honor God with words and confession, and then we rejoice! This is Biblical. We're told to rejoice. So go through life singing and praising and being giddy in the Lord. Let people wonder why you're smiling—you have a great reason!

"Look to the Lord and His strength; seek His face always," verse 11. One of the points I like about this verse, is that there aren't any hindrances. It doesn't say, "when you're upset," or "when the enemy strikes." It just tells us, all day every day, to "look to the Lord and

---

[1] Easton's Bible Dictionary
[2] Easton's Bible Dictionary

His strength." If we truly did that, and the following part, "seek His face always," would be ever have a bad day again? Would we ever get involved in an altercation or verbal assault? Can we be negative or frustrated or angry if we're truly looking to the Lord and His strength, and seeking His face? If we obeyed nothing but this verse for the rest of the day, week, month, and year, our entire life would be changed, beginning this afternoon. Don't look at how long your to-do list is, look at how short this verse is. The Lord will get you through your day, just look to Him and His strength. Don't look for short cuts at work or what someone can do for you, "seek His face." When you do that, you'll want to serve and esteem others (Philippians 2:3).

Okay, if verse 11 is too much to remember, then verse 12 offers one word for you: Remember. "Remember the wonders He has done, His miracles, and the judgments He pronounced." Again, when we get angry, or busy, or distracted, or fearful, or distraught, or upset, or any other negative emotion out there, if we could remember—that God is in control; that God loves us exactly where we are; that God is the great provider—if we would remember that we're sinful, and even so God sent Jesus to die on the cross so that we can live in heaven for eternity—that pretty much puts things in perspective.

Have you ever been going through a bad time—unemployment, divorce, a tough move, children's problems—when you hear about a family losing a child? Boy does that put your challenges in perspective! You can Praise the Lord on a whole new level that unemployment doesn't last. You can appreciate that compassion and mercy may be borne out of a tough move, and there's an opportunity to grow and mature, and be completely glad in your circumstance, because suddenly, not that much is being asked of you. Not in comparison to losing a child. That's remembering. Remembering to count the blessings we have (see above!); Remembering that this life is all about loving Christ and others, in that order; Remembering that this is all temporary, but heaven is eternal.

David wrote a beautiful song of thanksgiving hundreds of years ago, and it's still true today. The first thing David did was acknowledge, thank, and praise the Lord.  It's a great model for prayer for us today.  In a few verses, and a few words, you can live this model of prayer, starting today. My prayers go with you, dear Saints.

(October 2009)

# Quiet Time

Ah, Spring is here, Summer is coming, school is ending.  That joyful . . . lazy . . . quiet?  . . . s-t-r-e-s-s-f-u-l time of year when kids are home, the sun is hot, a/c is running but you're not.  Every year I come into this season thinking such wonderful thoughts—reading with my kids, ice cream on the deck, barbecues, and beach parties.  And all those things happen, but not necessarily how I imagined them.  I hate to admit how often I hear things coming out of my mouth that make me cringe, and how much more I would like to hear a calm, serene voice, that my children would actually pay attention to, instead.

Well, step one toward serenity would be, in my book, taking a quiet time for myself daily.  Now, literally EVERY class/seminar/session/sermon I have EVER heard on quiet time ALWAYS (can you get the point here) states to have quiet time first thing in the morning.  And I have.  For years I read and prayed first.  And if that works for you, all the better.  I see the point of it.  There were days when I read a verse that hit me so hard that it stayed with me all day, and at suppertime, I was ready to discuss it over a meal.

On the down side, however—in all those classes, downsides were rarely, if ever, mentioned—I found that when I started my day with my Bible, too often, by noon, I had lost my serenity. I'm pretty much of a morning girl, anyway, I had just slept for 6-8 hours (you can fill in your own time frame, and please don't be frustrated if yours doesn't match mine. My kids sleep through the night now), and I'm in a pretty good mood. I love mornings. The day is fresh, it's still cool, I have energy, my mind isn't cloudy, if I have a to-do list, it's already been written. So, I'm okay in the morning.

But when I move my quiet time to early afternoon, I find a plethora of benefits. First, it gets me back to a serene place, which is where I was already beginning each day. Second, it focuses me. I am being reminded to be like Christ, and by noon, I too often need that reminder. Third, once the kids were old enough to understand what I was doing, I was able to teach them that mommy's Bible reading is the most important thing I do every day. So, for this block of time, mommy needs you to stay focused on your work and/or play, and let mommy have my time. It was amazing how well they responded to this, even at a young age. And, I was modeling Bible study for them, in addition to receiving my quiet time.

So I am not advocating any time of day for quiet time, just that you do it, whenever it works for you. By the way, I learned that evening doesn't work for me, for a very specific reason. When I'm studying, I can really get excited about what I'm learning. So excited that I wouldn't be able to sleep. Now, some of you may be lulled to sleep in the Lord's arms if you do a late study, and I think that's a lovely lullaby, so again, learn what works for you.

Two ways to use your quiet time. Not that there are only two options out there, but for now, here are two ideas. One, let God talk to you; two, you talk to God. In the first, you would read your Bible, maybe take notes to journal, possibly use a study guide or commentary (check your local Christian bookstore), or just read. I firmly believe you can't read the same book in the Bible twice (hold on, I'm not done), because who you are when you read it, will change how you respond to it. So it's okay if you've read the Minor Prophets before, or it's your 3$^{rd}$ or 6$^{th}$ or 20$^{th}$ time through the gospels. Enjoy listening to the Lord. The Bible is new every day.

Talking to God is more about prayer, and is a lovely way to spend quiet time. Talk to Him. Tell Him you love Him. Imagine walking with Him, sitting with Him, laughing with Him—whatever works for you. Call Him Abba, or Adonai, or Jehovah Jirah, or whatever name you like, but call Him, at least once a day. Tell Him your fears (1 Peter 5:7), your dreams, your concerns, your joys. Think how much you like hearing from your children, and try to imagine how much more the Lord likes hearing your voice. He loves the sound of your voice, even your inner voice. And He's the only one in the universe who really hears you—your thoughts, ideas, nuances, and what you really mean and want to say. Cuddle up with the Lord daily, and have nice, long chats. Yes, you can give Him your list of prayer requests, the daily ones (safety and kindness for our children), and the long-reaching prayers (Christian spouses for children, preferably people with a very boring testimony).

Commit to having a daily quiet time this summer. You will reap a bountiful harvest from even a few minutes a day, and do it whenever it works for you. Read, talk, listen . . . just enjoy the solitude the Lord will allow, if you seek.
(June 2007)

# The Purpose of Storms

Storms come to everyone, no matter what you call them. Some call them tests, some call them challenges. For others, it's just life. Last Spring I heard a sermon in which I was told that the purpose of storms is to destroy my hope. Now, I have a more positive thought for the purpose of storms.

To appreciate storms, please know that we are, even as I type, feeling the effects of Hurricane Fay. The winds, rain, and clouds have been here for days, but they should end soon. Gustav is on the way. When a physical storm comes, people have a myriad of reactions. Some hide under the bed, figuratively. Others head outside to splash and smile. Some just ignore them, waiting them out until they can get back to their routine.

In this case, I welcomed Fay with open arms, not always my reaction to a physical storm. In the first place, the Lord has an amazing way of sending storms, like the tornado that came through our neighborhood last Spring, when my husband is out of town. Well, Rick has been here for this entire storm. But really, the joy of this storm for me is that, living in Georgia in August, it's supposed to be hot. Really hot. Mind-numbing, glowingly, hot. I like the heat. I like summer. But to have a respite of several days, with temperatures in the 70's, being able to wear pants just when I'm tired of shorts and tee-shirts, and knowing that it's a temporary situation, I was able to throw out my arms and hug the weather. Knowing it's temporary is key to why I was able to enjoy the storm. Besides, we really didn't have it too bad where I live, as Fay caused no local accidents.

Okay, so what about storms in our lives that are less physical? Joblessness, marriage challenges, children's problems, financial difficulties. These are all storms. How we view them and how we react can mean a huge difference in our daily walk and our testimony to others.

In spending time thinking about these storms, as, just like you, I've been through what feels like more than my share, I believe one reason the Lord allows them is to test our strength. Are we strong enough to hold up under the pressure? I hope not! We're told to rely on His strength (Phil 4:13), not our own. Now, as we mature in our faith, we should be faster to confide in the Lord and ask for His support.

In the same way, storms test our endurance. After we've been at this a while, this thing called life, we learn that good and bad come to everyone. Well, even now I'm going through a storm with my work, and I feel like I'm at the end of my endurance. How long does this have to last? I know the Lord could end it any second, if He only would. Of course, Scripture has a better answer for me, in Romans 15:4 – "For everything that was written in the past was written to teach us, so that through endurance and the encouragement of the Scriptures we might have hope." So as I endure, I have hope. I also know, through years of practice and training, that His timing really is perfect. Maybe the current or next storm is meant to improve your endurance. Those Olympians we saw last month didn't get that good overnight. It took years of training.

Your latest storm may be a test of your faith. I went through that one a few years ago. I just cried in the shower (my favorite place to cry) and thought that I just wasn't sure anymore. Well, PTL I only sat on the fence for a day before I realized how absurd I was being. Of course my God was greater than my circumstances. At first I was embarrassed to have even questioned, but then I realized, since I did come down on the right side, that God understood.

My last thought is that the storm may be allowed to test your flexibility. Oh, my, is this one again for me. I was incredibly legalistic growing up. Right was right, no discussion. I was frustrated and angry when I saw people get away with something, while I now realize that others, more mature than I was at the time, were merely being flexible. Can you flex when plans change? Sometimes the storm is sent to turn you in a new direction, just like a ship on the sea that seems to be going off course, but instead discovers new lands. And when you look out your window during the next windy day, see how well those mighty oaks sway in the breeze, but stand firm in their roots. Flexibility doesn't mean giving up your basic beliefs, it allows for some changes around the edges.

An important point in all these possible reasons for storms is that the word test is used in all of them. Now, whether or not you liked school, and whether or not you were a good student, and whether or not you excelled at test-taking, the point of the test is actually intended to be positive. A test allows you to show your knowledge. Think about a class you enjoyed, and in which you did excel. Those tests weren't bad. In fact, you felt good going in, and good coming out. And when you were the best in the class, that felt pretty darn good, too. A test is for our good, to show what we can do, not to trip us up and fail us, as is too often perceived.

So now the question is, how do you respond in a storm? Do you run into the middle of it, laughing and telling the sky to bring it on?  Could you?  Do you hide inside, cringing until it's over?  Do you calmly and patiently wait it out, knowing that storms simply can't last forever?  Can you make a decision now to change your reaction to storms?  Or, if your behavior is already excellent in this situation, can you teach others how to face a storm bravely?

We'll all face storms in our lives.  The Lord faced storms, and walked on water through one windy night to get to the boat and His friends (Matthew 14:26).  He also commanded the wind to be still, and it OBEYED (Mark 4:39).  Now, if the Lord can silence the wind in a storm, surely He's able to handle whatever storm you face. Let's commit to face our storms firmly standing by Jesus' side, so together we need never fear a storm again.  It will pass.

(September 2008)

# Create, An Attribute of God

The first action God took, in all of history, was to create. The first thing He did was to get to work. Genesis 1:1—"In the beginning, God **created** the heavens and the earth."

He didn't look for a snack or hit the couch, and not because He had yet to create them. As our perfect example, the first thing our Lord chose to do was create—work.

Note that create suggests imagination and creativity. He didn't choose the word build for this Scripture. God did, in fact, build the heavens and earth. And He built them out of nothing—nothing but His imagination and energy.

There's a thought. Did creating the world require energy? I think so, based on Genesis 2:2-3. We learn here that God rested. You don't get tired from sleeping—that refreshes you. But activity, whether work or fun, tires us. So, yes, God was expending energy from His activity of creating.

Obviously work tires us. Spend a day building a playground, cleaning a basement or garage, or hosting a garage sale. These are all physical efforts, but I'm guessing that creating animals, seas, and mountains could be considered physical effort as well.

Even mental work is tiring. Consider how exhausting it can be to spend an hour, only an hour, paying bills and reconciling a checkbook. Students, doesn't it tire your brain to read a new chapter, especially of an unfamiliar, and possibly uninteresting to you, topic? And I can't be the only person who needs a break after a session of Scripture memorization.

And more energy can be required to play. Go outside and play two-hand touch football with the neighborhood kids. Treat yourself to a day of window-shopping. Volunteer to play with the babies in the nursery. You'll be tired, and you might be breathless immediately upon completing any given activity.

So, yes, activity can tire us out. But what a great feeling!

Questions: What was the last creative activity in which you took part? What creative work would you like to begin now?

I remember coming home from church one Sunday when my kids were young(er). It was a cold and dreary January day. The holidays were over and the New Year's routine was just beginning. I sat down on the couch with the newspaper and an afghan and felt crummy. Not bad, but not good—a general malaise. I couldn't get warm and I just felt icky.

Then our neighbor came over. He had decided to throw a surprise birthday party for his wife, to be held in four hours. Could we help? Could we!

We planned and quickly made lists—people to call, groceries to purchase, decorations to find. Two of us headed to the store and one got on the phone.

Not only did the party come off beautifully, but it energized me! Without a motivator, I might have spent a cold day on the couch.  Instead, I was put to work.  It was the best thing that could have happened to me.

Questions:  Have you ever had more energy after a physical activity?  If so, describe the situation.  Can you use this to motivate you in future?

**What to Create?**

Okay, we're supposed to create, but what?  This is not only a personal issue, but a timely issue.  As children, we are encouraged to create anything with anything.  A picture with paints (to be proudly displayed on the refrigerator), a building with toothpicks and glue, a plant stand with wood and nails.  See how the materials and tools mature with us?

As we grow, the ideas can get more complex and less tangible.  Now God created you, yourself, and He did a perfect job (Psalm 139:14-15).  What we create as adults is still a function of who we are and our season of life.  As a young married person, we create a good marriage; we create a happy, serene, accepting home; we create couple friendships, instead of same gender friendships.

As a parent, we create a healthy environment for children to thrive.  A math-type or engineer might write it as follows:

F(child) = time, love, Bible, attention

Using time, love, the Bible, and attention we create a healthy, happy, well-adjusted, God-respecting Christian person.  Once our children are grown we don't stop being creative, we just change our focus.  Once God made the kangaroo, He didn't stop making animals.  He still had a lot of ideas for heads and tails and legs.  But after making two kangaroos, one male and one female, they were capable of reproducing themselves, just like our children.  So God might have moved on to the Koala bear (there's nothing to suggest that the Lord created animals alphabetically), all the way down to the Zebra. So, what do we create?

Questions:  What have you created in your early years, teen years, middle years, later years?

Your list might look like this:

| Early years | Teen years | Middle years | Later years |
|---|---|---|---|
| Clay bowls | Friendships | Family | Laughter |
| Coloring | Hurt feelings | Memories | Paintings |
| Wooden bin | x-stitches | Rebuilt cars | Scrapbooks |

A lot of what you create will be a continuous creation, such as friendships or kindness.  You'll watch it, nourish it, and encourage its growth as a creator.  Other things might seem more temporary—a retreat or Bible study you coordinate.  But even while the experience itself may be gone, it continues to live in you because you grow with each of your creations.

**How to create**
So how can we be creative and get to work? Scripture doesn't say specifically that God had a plan before making the world, but I'm guessing He knew what He was doing before He began.  I mean, He didn't make any critters before He had places for them to live.
Please read Genesis 1:9-27 then answer the following questions.
On what day did God create the sea?_____
On what day did God create marine life?_____
On what day did God create mountains?_____
On what day did God create mountain goats?_____
On what day did God create us in His own image?_____

God allows us all to be unique in our own ways. That's why some are tall while others aren't; some are night owls, others are morning prowlers. Some are planners and others are wingers. First, determine who you are. Then, use your gifts to God's glory. (March 2008)

# The Prodigal Son

In Luke 15:11, Jesus begins telling the story of the prodigal son.  My daughter's newer Bible has the subtitle, The Parable of the Lost Son.  He was definitely lost, and he was a prodigal.  As defined by Mirriam-Webster, a prodigal is "characterized by profuse or wasteful expenditure; lavish outlays for clothes; recklessly spendthrift."  Let's look at the story, in little pieces, so we can really appreciate what the Lord is telling us.  You can use your own Bible, or follow along with the verses as I offer them.

Verse 11:  "Jesus continued."  Let's stop.  Jesus has already been teaching, and if we look above, we'll see He's shared the parable of the Lost Sheep and the Lost Coin.  In both these parables, and remember that a parable was a story with a moral principle in it, Jesus is making the point that He will do anything, even things that neighbors might consider loony, to save even one of His children.  So, now we know what He's been saying, let's see what He says next:

Jesus continued:  "There was a man who had two sons.  The younger one said to his father, "Father, give me my share of the estate." So he divided his property between them."

Let's stop. Okay, two sons. But in this world, was it the norm for the younger son to receive the same inheritance as the older son? No. The oldest, heir, was often the preferred son. But in this case, the son felt comfortable enough to go to his father and ask—hm, maybe a bit stronger than ask—demand, maybe? Basically, he wanted what he thought was coming to him, and he didn't want to wait for his dad to die. Isn't that a lovely thought?

How would you feel if your children came to you and said, "Listen, you know I get a percentage when you die, anyway, but I want it now. I don't even need it for a new business or home or food for my children. I just want to live well on what you've worked for." How would you respond?

The father (by the way, I think some very kind adjectives could be used here, like generous, kind, and patient, but I digress)—the father "divided his property between them." This suggests he gave the older son his inheritance, too. Very generous. Let's continue.

Verse 13: "Not long after that (an hour, maybe? A day?), the younger son got together all he had, set off for a distant country, and there squandered his wealth in wild living."

Let's look at this: the boy takes the money, and runs far, far away. Away from everyone who might know him. And then, he lives wildly. We can use our imagination regarding what that might suggest.

Verse 14: "After he had spent everything," Stop. Please note the word everything. His father gave him half his estate, the child's full inheritance, and he spent it ALL. Everything! Did the child have no self control? It took his father a lifetime to build up that wealth, and it was all gone.

Continuing, "there was a severe famine in that whole country, and he began to be in need." See, it wasn't his fault. The entire country was in a famine.

Verse 15: "So he went and hired himself out to a citizen of that country, who sent him to his fields to feed pigs." Stop.

Some good irony is entering this story. First, because he had traveled far from home, and he never had any real friends in this place, he didn't have anywhere to go. And humans do have an amazing sense of survival, so he knew he had to work, possibly for the first time in his life, since he was raised as the owner's son. But, he's put to work feeding pigs. It's a fair assumption that the family in the story is Jewish, so the fact that he was sent to feed pigs is an especially rude insult. And, continuing the story, this poor child is ready to eat the pigs' food:

Verse 16: "He longed to fill his stomach with the pods that the pigs were eating, but no one gave him anything." He was living worse than pigs, which weren't even kosher for him. That's an amazing insult! It's okay, good stuff is coming.

Verse 17: "When he came to his senses," Stop. Coming to his senses obviously took a trip, because it was someplace he had to go. He had to come to his senses, like he wasn't immediately there. Amazing.

"When he came to his senses, he said, "How many of my father's hired servants have food to spare, and here I am starving to death!"" Notice the exclamation point. He's getting it! And he's getting angry. Now we know why it was important for him to be far away from his family, otherwise his father's land would be in a famine, too. There's another reason coming up, too, and this is excellent foreshadowing.

"I will set out and go back to my father and say to him: Father, I have sinned against heaven and against you. I am no longer worthy to be called your son; make me like one of your hired servants."

Yes! Humility. He understands. He messed up big time, and he has a plan, where first he apologizes, then he humbly asks to be a servant. But, it's easy to make our plans, and sometimes harder to see them through, true?

How many times, in the middle of the night, do we plan to rise early to study/have a quiet time/exercise; or how many promises do we make in the middle of the night to not raise our voice/hear out other people/respond and not react?  Don't be convicted. That's not the point. Let's see how the son does.

Verse 20:  "So he got up and went to his father." I think the immediacy of his actions speaks well of him.

Continuing:  "But while he was still a long way off, his father saw him and was filled with compassion for him; he ran to his son, threw his arms around him, and kissed him."

Excuse me?  Not only is this an AMAZING response to a bratty son, but there's so much more here. First, while the son was still a long way off, his father saw him.  I've been taught that this means the father had to have been looking for him.  Even though the son had to have been gone for months, as he traveled to a distant country (v.13), the father was still looking for him, hoping.  Oh, the joy of hope.

Second, he felt compassion.  Mirriam-Webster says compassion is "sympathetic consciousness of others' distress together with a desire to alleviate it; pity." Wow.  He could see his son's distress and wanted to stop it.  That's kindness.  Personally, I'd still be angry, and this father is feeling compassion.

Third, and this is hugely important, and PTL I learned it a long time ago, in College.  The father ran to his son.  In this world, what the son did was treasonous. The neighbors could have seen him and stoned him for even having the nerve to return.  They would have known about what he'd done, and it wouldn't have set well with them for a plethora of reasons.

So when the father ran to him, let's stop.  Ran. That's a word you think of with children and playing; or exercising and athletes. It's not a word you associate with the father of grown sons. And you don't associate it with a respectable business man. But, by running to his son, this father could have saved his son's life. Remember, the neighbors could have stoned the child for his behavior. But the father couldn't have that. He wouldn't have that. He had waited for this day, and couldn't even wait for his son to make it all the way home, but ran to him and welcomed him home, saving his life by doing so.

Another thing to consider, the son was probably filthy. He'd been traveling a great distance, without money, which means he walked on dusty, unpaved roads, probably in warm temperatures, after working with pigs, so when the father hugged and kissed him, the son was probably a smelly, sweaty mess. That's love.

Now, we all know that in this parable, our God is the Father, and we are the son. We're the bratty, selfish, egocentric child. I can relate to that. I still have a hard time wrapping my mind around the idea of how much God loves me and will do for me, including not just risking death, but dying!

But the story isn't over. The son, having come to his senses, has a job to do. Let's keep going.

The son is now going to give his speech, and in fact, in verse 21, "The son said to him, "Father, I have sinned against heaven and against you. I am no longer worthy to be called your son.""

What does the Bible say will happen when we are humble? We all know that pride goeth before the fall; do you know that humility goes before honor (Proverbs 15:33 and Matthew 23:12)? And that's what happened!

The father didn't want to hear apologies or stories. He was just so tickled to have his baby home that he wanted to throw a party, and he did. Now, we know there were still challenges with the older brother, and we can probably relate. I mean, the spoiled baby takes advantage and gets a party, while he gets nothing? That's how much God loves you. No matter what you

have done, or will do, He will run to you as soon as you turn to Him.  If you haven't turned to Him yet, if you've never asked Jesus to be your personal Savior, if you don't have a personal relationship with the Trinity, take a minute now to admit you're a prodigal, state your belief that Jesus' blood saved you from hell, and confess your sins to Him.  He loves you, dear one, and is waiting for you to turn, so He can run to you!
(November 2008)

# Stewardship

Lest you fear that this is going to be another opportunity for someone to tell you to give, give, give, please let me put your mind at rest. While money is mentioned, this is not a financial article. Whew!

We are, however, talking about tithing, and to do that, we have to turn to Malachi 3:10, which says in the NIV, "Bring the whole tithe into the storehouse, that there may be food in My house. Test me in this," says the Lord Almighty, "and see if I will not throw open the floodgates of heaven and pour out so much blessing that you will not have room enough for it."

This is what some teachers would call a pregnant sentence. I mean, there's a lot there! The first point I want to make is that the tithe is never requested until AFTER we have been BLESSED. We are to bring one tenth (a tithe) of the harvest to the Lord, but not until after the harvest. That means if we harvest nothing, we give the Lord nothing. If we gather little, we share little. It's when we are greatly blessed that we have a large tithe. Now, this seems more than fair when you look at it rationally. The Lord asks for nothing unless and until He blesses our work, then He allows us to keep 90% of what is, actually, His, and asks us for only 10%. An agent in Hollywood wouldn't give you so great a deal.

But, before we move on, let's look carefully at the verse. It says to bring the **whole** tithe. This means, don't try to shortchange the Lord. If anybody knows the truth, our omnipotent Lord does! He sees all and knows all, and after all, He's only asking for 10%. And I'm guessing you've heard it said that the Lord can do more with your 90% than you can do with the entire 100%. Then, THEN, the Lord instructs us **in the Bible** to TEST HIM!

How many of us like to be tested? We even teach new Christians not to pray for patience, because the Lord will test our patience, and we don't want that! Now think back to school days (for some of us this is a longer trip), and those tests. But, thinking back, the tests I didn't fear were the ones that I truly prepared for. Well, the Lord is prepared. He asks us, encourages us, even commands us to TEST HIM. Let's do it! Let's agree to give our 10%, or more, and see if the Lord isn't good for His word—remember, we have chapter and verse to claim here. We all know He's going to pass the test, but let's be obedient and test Him.

So since this isn't a financial article, let's get to stewardship. First, let's look at Mark 4:24 and see what stewardship ISN'T. In the NIV it reads, "Consider carefully what you hear," He (Jesus) continued. "With the measure you use, it will be measured to you—and even more."

I was taught at some point early in my life that this was directly related to how much I gave the church, a person in need, or even the homeless on the streets of DC, where I lived as a young adult. I was told on a Sunday morning that the Lord was watching me daily (true), and that if I didn't give to the homeless, then heaven wouldn't welcome me (untrue). I was a very young Christian, but mature enough to know that giving to the homeless is not how to gain entry to heaven. (It's about a personal relationship with Jesus, and it's an article unto itself, but you can look up Romans 10:9 and John 14:6 for a quick explanation of how to gain heaven if you're unsure of your own salvation.  Or contact me—I LOVE to talk about this!)

So if this isn't what Mark 4:24 is saying, what does it mean?  This verse is talking about the measure of study we do, and how much wisdom we can gain.  The more time we put into Bible study, prayer, and fellowship with the trinity will determine our growth, maturity, and wisdom.  Isn't that logical and loving and much more suited to our loving Father than the idea that He'll withhold His blessings if we don't do things His way? Looking back, I don't understand how this verse could ever be misunderstood, but it is.

Okay, still knowing this article isn't about finances, and knowing what stewardship isn't, let's look beyond finances.  I have five (5!) ideas of things that require attention and stewardship.  They are time, space, talents, possessions, and energy.

First, are you tithing your time?  The Lord gives us all 24 hours a day.  Some of those days I know I spend well, others I don't.  Some people think they have to have a thirty minute quiet time every day at 5:00 a.m. If that works for them, and you, that's great!  But, the more we invest our time, the more the Lord promises to bless it and return it to us.  So, if I commit 10% of every day to the Lord, I can get more done in the remaining 90%.  How to give the Lord your time?  Prayer, service, and Bible study are all quick answers.  The prayer can be done as you go about your day, although there's no substitute for taking some alone time with the Lord. You'll be greatly rewarded for this alone time where it's only you and the Trinity.  Service isn't just feeding the homeless.  It's serving your family, neighbors, teachers, colleagues, or wherever you are in life.

Yesterday after class one of my students told me he wanted to do something nice during class, but the moment passed and he didn't do it. I told him to never miss an opportunity to do a nice thing, because the opportunity may never come again. Even hearing about it afterwards isn't the same as the spontaneity of the moment. He could have greatly blessed someone, and he missed the opportunity. Bless the people with whom you come into contact daily as part of your time tithe, with a kind word, genuine compliment, or taking time to help someone.

Space? Yes, space. If you're anything like me, as an American, I must consume about twemty times the world's norm in having a home far larger than the majority of people in the world. Do I feel bad about this? No. The Lord has blessed us, and we've done our best to return the blessing. When the church asks for someone to house visiting missionaries for a night, weekend, or month, try to say yes, even if it's inconvenient.

When our church asked for housing for a visiting choir, we only had a guest room, while friends were offering a finished basement with a private bath. But you know what? Our guest room was needed and we had a lovely girl spend a few nights with us, and we were the ones blessed. We provided a room, and I offered her the use of our washer and dryer, which she gratefully accepted. She left us with a tape of her music, and lovely memories. And we only gave up a couple nights of an unused room! A friend with a private pool is very quick to offer to host parties at her home. Everybody loves it, and the Lord loves her heart.

Share the space in your car, and drive someone on errands, or to church, or wherever they're going. I know the price of gas seems outrageously high, but wouldn't that be a great blessing, to have the Lord bless the gas mileage in your car? He can do it!

Let's talk about talents. For some of you, this is easy. You sing at church, you're active at community events. If someone calls you, you're there and ready to help. For some of us, who completely missed the line when vocal and physical talents were being handed out, it's harder, because nobody comes looking for our abilities—or do they?  Has someone asked recently for Sunday School children's teachers?  There are some people who are called to that ministry, and some people who couldn't last ten minutes in that room.  You know your likes and dislikes—find them and use them to serve the Lord. If you knit, donate items to a shelter.  If you're an organizer, offer your help to the church, or school, or even friends.  If you can paint a wall, and you know somebody who needs their house painted, pick up the phone and offer your services. It's not just about writing a check, but using the talents and abilities the Lord has chosen to bless you.

Let's practice stewardship with our possessions. The above example of house and car take care of both time and space, but let's share more of our possessions. I'm not asking you to give away 10% of what you own, but let's share what we have. Years ago, when a girl complimented a pin I was wearing several times, I took it off and gave it to her.  I promise she received much more joy from that pin than I did—so why have I not done the same with more of my possessions?  Maybe because nobody seems to want what I have, but probably because I haven't listened to the prompting of the Holy Spirit to do so.  What a blessing you could be to someone by sharing a sandwich at lunchtime, offering to buy somebody a soda just to be kind, or bringing extra dessert to the office. Yes, it took you time and effort, and yes, your family would love to have the extra dessert, but what a blessing you will be to others when you live beyond yourself.

Finally, let's tithe our energy.  Stewardship goes so much further than just writing a check on Sunday morning, and stewardship on energy is something that can be done daily.  Get up a little early to make a nice breakfast for your family.  You will all be so blessed, and the day will start so much nicer, that you may decide to make it a regular event. Time in the morning, even while cooking, is a wonderful time to be alone with the Lord to start your day. The next time you reach for something fun, whether it's a book, the computer, or whatever your hobby is, put it down and do something nice for someone. You could both bless them and surprise them! They might even reciprocate to you or someone else, which passes the blessing on. At work or school, where can you spend a little energy to make someone else's life easier? Carry their burden as the Lord carries yours. In your community or church, you may have to look for the right opportunity, but there are people out there waiting for you to call them.

Years ago, my then 6th grade daughter got interested in pageants when she read Heather Whitestone's autobiography. So I called the city to ask about their Miss Pageant, and was told they were short of help. So I offered to help, so that my daughter might be able to follow her dream—I thought it was rather selfish of me. The next thing I knew, I was completely in charge of the program. I ran the program for two years, until we moved to another state. There was definitely a need, but I had to go looking for it, and the Lord lead me to it through my daughter. Boy, He sure has His ways!

You don't even have to tithe your time, energy, or talents in formal ways. Grab a trash bag and head for the nearest city park. Nobody is going to get mad at a citizen collecting trash. You might get some odd looks, and people might incorrectly think this is your job, but you and the Lord know the truth. You'll be showing good stewardship of your time and abilities, and the Lord will be watching from heaven, not to bless you with entry, but just smiling at you. He really loves you just as you are!

(May 2008)

# How Jesus Handled Bullies

Have you ever felt crummy, like everyone was after you? People at work are picking on you, friends are letting you down, even your own mom has less than nice things to say to you? Okay, sometimes it's deserved and for our own good, but other times we KNOW it's not us. Sometimes there are bullies out there. The sad part is that they can be disguised as teachers, friends, even family members. The question is, how to handle bullies?

Well, you may have never thought about it, but Jesus was badly treated long before the cross. He was bullied by people He didn't know, He was bullied by religious people, and He was even bullied by His family. They said some unkind things about Him. Let's look at what was said, and how Jesus responded.

First let's go to Mark, chapter 5, where Jesus was asked to heal a little girl, but appeared to get there late. We'll start at verse 38: "when they came to the home of the synagogue ruler, Jesus saw a commotion, with people crying and wailing loudly. He went in and said them, "Why all this commotion and wailing? The child is not dead, but asleep." Verse 40 (emphasis mine): *"BUT THEY LAUGHED AT HIM."*

These are people the Lord didn't know. Jesus was there at the girl's father's request, and when He shows up and makes a statement, people start laughing at Him. Now, wouldn't that just crush you? I mean, you come into a group of people, say something, and they start laughing at you. My! I would turn around and go home, deciding to never return again and never do anything nice again. Praise the Lord, not our Jesus.

What did Jesus do? Verse 40 continues and tells us, He went about His business: "After He put them all out, He took the child's father and mother and the disciples who were with Him, and went in where the child was. He took her by the hand and said to her, "Talitha koum! (which means, "Little girl, I say to you, get up!").

Jesus didn't worry about the laughter. He was there to do a job, and He did it. He didn't pay any attention to the laughter, or those laughing, at all—easier for Him, maybe, but we're all called to be Christ-like. When you're about your business, especially if it's serving the Lord, then go about your business, and don't let rude or inappropriate comments deter you.

Now let's go to John, chapter 10. Jesus is talking from the beginning of the chapter about The Shepherd and His Flock. He explains that He is the gate for the sheep (verse 7). He ends in verse 18 by saying, "No one takes it (life) from Me, but I lay it down of My own accord. I have authority to lay it down and authority to take it up again. This command I received from My Father."

Starting at verse 19, the following is said, "At these words the Jews were again divided. Many of them said, "He is demon-possessed and raving mad. Why listen to Him?"

Talk about fighting words! You may have been called names before—I know I've been called all kinds of mean things. But I don't think I was ever called demon-possessed. And the comment, "Why listen to Him?" OUCH! That would hurt anyone.

In this section, no response is recorded on Jesus' part, and I'm guessing that's because there wasn't one. I don't know that, but I find it hard to believe that if a great debate resulted, nobody commented on it, although it's possible. The lack of response is good enough for me. When bullied/teased/picked on—say nothing.

The final Scripture we visit today is Mark 3:21b. We'll start just before that, in verse 20, but get ready! "Then Jesus entered a house, and again a crowd gathered, so that He and His disciples were not even able to eat. When His family heard about this, they went to take charge of Him for they said, "He is out of His mind.""

The really amazing part of that verse to my mind, is that it was His family! Jesus was so popular that He couldn't even eat, but His family went to take charge of Him, as though He were a child or of a deranged mind. He didn't need to be taken care of! He was God's Son. He knew what He was doing. But, even His own family spoke unkindly about Him.

So, if you've been bullied or teased or harassed, what's the right thing to do? Well, Jesus' response was to ignore the laughter, to go about His business, and to do what He knew to do, which was obey the Lord. The next time something negative happens to you, can you try to ignore it, walk away from it, and go about your business? I'm sure it will take the wind out of the sails of those bothering you, and, as it says in 1 Peter 2:20, it will find favor with God.

(June 2008)

# When Life Gets Tough

When life gets tough, the tough get going, right?
When life gives you lemons, make lemonade, right?  The
adages are nice to hear, and said loudly and often
enough, they can even energize you, especially when
heard with a thousand of your best friends at a
Motivational Seminar.  I know.  I'm one of the many
Motivational Speakers out there.  A major difference
between the Motivational Seminars I give, and the
Christian Seminars I give, is Scripture.  Both types of
seminars are moral, encouraging, and uplifting.

When life gets hard, we need to return to simple
truths.  It's good to get back to basics.  That's what
we're here to do today.

First, I know the economy is harsh right now.  I
hear and read the stories about what a pickle we have
gotten ourselves into as a nation.  This isn't the first time
we've been here, and unless Jesus comes back soon, it
may not be the last.  The last time the economy was
worse than it is today was only a generation ago.  No, we
don't have to go back to the 1930's when the 1970's,
with double digit inflation and double digit
unemployment, is far enough of a trip.  Even the
recession of 1980-81 was worse in some ways than

where we are today.  We need to remember, and remind ourselves daily, that God is our source—not our employers, not the government, certainly not the welfare system, or the spending bill enacted last month.  God is our only source.

Before I point out just a very, very minor portion of Scripture below, I have to tell you what a blessing writing this article has been.  Like everyone, I have better and worse days, but you can't have a bad day when you're spending it in the Bible.  Okay, here we go.

When trouble comes, we can fight or flee.  I think if we choose to flee, we should run, and I mean literally, to Scripture.  I've accumulated some Scripture to assure all of us that God is still in His heaven, and all is still right with the world (with thanks to Robert Browning).

First, let's look at some of the promises the Lord has made to us.  Then we'll look at what our response should be.  In several of the references the two are intertwined, as though the Lord KNEW we were going to need them to be written that way. My gosh, we do.

In Malachi 3:6, God says, "I, the Lord, do not change.  So you, O descendants of Jacob, are not destroyed."  Let's just concentrate on the first sentence.  The Lord does not change.  This concept is repeated throughout Scripture.  God is the same, no matter who or what government is in power in every country on earth.  God is still in control.  He doesn't change, and won't change.  We can count on Him.  We can count on Him to love us and care for us.

Chances are good that you've heard the quote from Hebrews 13:5 – "Never will I leave you; never will I forsake you."  You may have believed, because it's a New Testament quote, that it was said by Jesus.  In fact, the unknown writer of Hebrews was quoting Deuteronomy, verses 6 and 8 of chapter 31.  It's important to return to the Old Testament to study the quote.  Both of the quotes intertwine God's actions and ours, as promised above, and they flip the order.  First, we're told to be strong, courageous, and unafraid, because God won't leave us: Deuteronomy 31:6 – "Be strong and courageous. Do not be afraid or terrified because of them, for the Lord your God goes with you; He will never leave you nor forsake you." Then, we're reminded, only two verses later, that because God will always be with us, we need to not be afraid or discouraged: Deuteronomy 31:8 – "The Lord Himself goes before you and will be with you; He will never leave you nor forsake you. Do not be afraid; do not be discouraged."

When Scripture repeats itself so quickly, such as when Jesus would say, "Verily, verily", that means pay attention, this is really, really important. And it is! The writer, Moses, was obedient to repeat this promise of the Lord. We, as children, need to hear the promise and our part repeated in order to really get it.

We're okay. We don't need to be afraid or dismayed by what's going on in Congress, on Wall Street, and in the economy. Further, we should be strong and courageous. Don't back down, Saints. We're on the side of right. God is with us through every worry, every financial question, every unemployment. God takes care of the birds of the air and the lilies and of the field, and you, dear saints, are so much more important than these (Matthew 6). They weren't created in God's image, but you are!

Let's continue. We like to have some image of being in control, even though when it comes to eternity, we have none. But on this earth, in our families, at work, we do seem to have some control, at least over our own actions. So let's see what Scripture tells us in just a few places. First, turn to Matthew 6:33, because it's there we learn the very first thing we're to do: "Seek first His kingdom and His righteousness, and all these things will be given to you as well." See, we're told to FIRST seek the Lord. We have some more things to do, but only after we've sought the Lord. Then the Lord gives us a promise right there in the same first: "AND all these things WILL BE added" (emphasis mine). It's an if-then loop, for you computer people out there. We seek, the Lord adds blessings to our lives. Too cool!

Other things for us to do come from both the Old Testament and New Testament. Psalm 37:4 tells us, "Delight yourself in the Lord and He will grant you the desires of your heart." Again, a promise is given with our job. When we delight ourselves in the Lord—when we praise Him for the blessings we receive, even if the blessing is uncomfortable—He will give us the desires of our heart. It may not be evident that losing a job is a blessing, but if you're walking with the Lord, you know His ways are not our ways. So praise Him for the job loss, because He has something better planned for you. Praise Him for the financial difficulties, although you may not understand it. It may not be easy or fun right now, but we all know that God's timing isn't the same as ours, either.

Let's think about that. Remember, we're babies to the Lord. Our minds will never come near His. Think about a child's ways compared to the mama's ways. The child wants the cookie, but the mama wants the baby to have healthier food, at least first. The child wants to stay up late, but the mama knows the child needs his rest. From that perspective, is it easier to accept that the Lord's timing is probably better than ours? He's not trying to keep us from what we see as the good stuff, He's giving it to us when we can best handle it. As adults, we do get to eat the cookies, because we know to have a meal first; and we do get to stay up later, which is hilarious because we want to go to bed earlier.

In the New Testament, Philippians 4:6 – "Be anxious about nothing, but in all things, through prayer and supplication, with thanksgiving, present your requests to the Lord." Okay, now we're being told not just what to do, but what not to do. Yes, we give thanks (in all circumstances, if you look at 1 Thessalonians

5:18); and yes, we pray and ask. But we're also told to stop worrying—"Be anxious about nothing." Nothing! No thing. There is nothing going on in your life of which God is unaware. He knows you're worried about the value of your home. He knows you need to put your child through College. He knows your car is giving you trouble. Stop worrying about it! Peter tells us to "cast all our cares upon Him, for He cares for you." There it is twice, and that's off the top of my head. Go on a scavenger hunt through the Bible, and you will find a veritable treasure of wonderful promises.

But we're not done yet, although that would have been a good conclusion. There's so much more, even with the few verses I've chosen, and I can't even get through those. I'll add some more verses to the end of the article that you can review on your own. But I do need to wrap this up. Stay with me for two more verses, please, dear Saints.

Again from the Old Testament, Psalm 118:6-7 – "The Lord is with me, I will not be afraid. What can man do to me? The Lord is with me; He is my helper. I will look in triumph on my enemies." That's it! That's why we came to the Lord. We can't get through this life well without Him! He is with you, so you don't need to be concerned about anything!

When anybody you don't know tells you that they want to take care of you, in today's world, you need to ask, "What do they want from me?" They may want to make a sale, they may want your vote. But you know the Lord. When He says He is with us, it's only because He enjoys being with us. What a blessing! He doesn't need anything from you, because He has it all. And He actually wants to, and can, take care of your needs and desires.

One more stop in the New Testament: Hebrews 13:6 – So we say with confidence, "The Lord is my helper, I will not be afraid. What can man do to me?" Yes, we're just quoting the Old Testament here. Some messages are so important that they have to be repeated, especially as these letters were targeting different audiences.  But you, dear Christian, are the intended reader of both.

Say it out loud when you're having a really bad day.  Even shout it!  "The Lord is my helper. I will NOT be afraid.  What can man do to me?"  I said it aloud as I typed it.  I'll say it again.  There.  It puts what I'm hearing on the radio, about the economy, in perspective. (March 2009)

More Scriptures you may want to check out:

Malachi 3:7 – "Ever since the time of your forefathers you have turned away from My decrees and have not kept them.  Return to Me, and I will return to you," says the Lord Almighty."

Psalm 3:5,6 – "Lean not on your own understanding.  In all your ways acknowledge Him and He will make your paths straight."

Psalm 121:1-8 - "I lift up my eyes to the hills—where does my help come from?  My help comes from the Lord, the Maker of heaven and earth. He will not let your foot slip—He who watches over you will not slumber; Indeed, He who watches over Israel will neither slumber nor sleep. The Lord watches over you—the Lord is your shade at your right hand. The sun will not harm you by day, nor the moon by night. The Lord will keep you from all harm—He will watch over your life; The Lord will watch over your coming and going both now and forevermore."

Psalm 100:1-5 "Shout for joy to the Lord, all the earth. Worship the Lord with gladness, come before Him with joyful songs. Know that the Lord is God.  It is He who made us, and we are His, we are His people, the sheep of His pasture. Enter His gates with thanksgiving and His courts with praise; give thanks to Him and praise His name. For the Lord is good and His love endures forever; His faithfulness continues through all generations."

# Jesus is Light

Who likes darkness? Bats. Who likes to be in the darkness? Sleeping people. Who prefers darkness over light? That's a question for you. What do you think of when you hear the word light? Do you think of the sun, the brightest star in the sky? Do you think of light bulbs? We can determine where the lamp goes and how bright it might be, by choosing the wattage for the bulb in the lamp. Think of light we sing about: Sunshine on My Shoulders; This Little Light of Mine; I'm Walking on Sunshine. Do you think of lightness versus darkness? In a dark room, any light at all can be considered very bright when it's first turned on. Do you know that Jesus and others often referred to Him as light?

I like John 8:12, which reads, "When Jesus spoke again to the people, He said, "I am the light of the world. Whoever follows Me will never walk in darkness, but will have the light of life.""

Wow, what a promise! He is the light of the world—not of the room, or a city, or state, or even a country, but the entire globe. That's something. Do you think it's accidental that son and sun are homonyms?

Isn't there an adage about it being better to light a single candle than to curse the darkness? Do you ever do that? Aren't you sure you can maneuver from your bedroom to the bathroom without a light, but then you stub your toe? Wouldn't it have been better to flip on a light? What keeps us from wanting the help of the light? Pride? Cheapness at paying for ten seconds of electricity? Concern about disturbing others? It doesn't really matter, as the point is, turn to the light.

That's another thing. We've all seen that bugs are attracted to light. Aren't most humans also attracted to people who eschew light? Certainly thousands of people were attracted to Jesus while He walked the earth, and millions have come to Him since He died, was buried, and rose again (1 Corinthians 15:3-4). Aren't you more attracted to people who seem to be brighter than those who seem dark?

Think of someone whom, upon first meeting, you wanted to get to know better. It may have been the first time you met a boy/girlfriend, but I'm thinking of someone of your own gender. When you met them for the first time, you just thought, "Wow, this person is fun. I'd like to spend more time with them." So you made plans to see them again, meet for lunch, or take in a movie together. Thus, a friendship was born. You don't try to begin a relationship with someone whom you find to be dark and negative, do you? Sometimes we find ourselves in those relationships anyway, but often we are the befriended in that relationship, not the one who instigates the friendship.

John spoke about Jesus being light in his gospel, his letters, and the Revelation. In John 1:4-5, he says, "In Him was life, and that life was the light of men. The light shines in the darkness, but the darkness has not understood it." Isn't that sad? Jesus was there, but was misunderstood by many of those on whom He shed His light. In 1 John 1:7, John wrote, "But if we walk in the light, as He is in the light, we have fellowship with one another, and the blood of Jesus, His Son, purifies us from all sin." And two verses later wrote, "The true light that gives light to every man was coming into the world."

So while others didn't recognize Jesus then, and millions don't recognize our need for Him as our Savior today, John is telling us very clearly Jesus is the light of the world, and that we can have fellowship with Him and other believers through Him.

Is this new to anyone? What if you want to believe, but just haven't learned how? Here's what John quotes Jesus as saying, in John 12:36, "Put your trust in the light while you have it, so that you may become sons of light." That was me for a long time. I thought I was a Christian years before I learned the truth of the need to have a personal relationship with Jesus and accept Him as my Savior. It's still the single best decision I've ever made.

So what does this talk of light do for believers? 1 Thessalonians 5:5 tells us, "You are all sons of the light and sons of the day. We do not belong to the night or to the darkness." I love that thought! We are of the day, when truth is revealed. I heard the line growing up in the south, "nothing good ever happens after midnight." I tried replying with, "We're not doing anything after midnight that we couldn't do before midnight." But the truth was, and is, there was more trouble started as the night got later. But as Christians, we don't belong to the night or to the darkness. What a blessing!

So how do we show the light of Christ to others, both believers and nonbelievers? There are dozens of ways, many of them common sensical. First, know your Bible. I had a friend once with whom I went out to lunch fairly regularly. One of us would always call the other the morning of the lunch, to confirm the time and place. I didn't realize that I tended to say something like, "I'll be able to leave as soon as I finish my Bible study," or, "Yes, I'm ready. I did my Bible study early today," until she pointed it out to me. By simply sharing my day with this friend I was witnessing to her that my Bible reading was important and I wanted it to be done before a lunch date.

Our language often alerts and encourages others of our beliefs. I know many people who sprinkle their conversation with phrases such as, "It was such a blessing," and "I had to praise the Lord when . . . " That's a sure way to let people know you recognize the source of all good gifts.

Most of all, our behavior needs to be light for those in the darkness. Do the right thing, even when you think nobody is watching. Be mannerly, polite, and overly kind. You may impress some people and shock others. Make it a point to respond in a tough situation, not just react. All of these ideas are full articles and lessons in themselves, I'm just trying to throw some ideas out there to encourage us to live our Christian lives. You can even be more proactive, writing a card, baking for someone, or sharing your time and talents.

Let's go in a new direction for a minute. Being me, I looked up definitions of light. I enjoy doing that. This is my favorite: "something that makes things visible or affords illumination" (dictionary.com). Doesn't that just fit our very definition of Christ? He makes things visible and affords illumination. I think that's why some people (think Pharisees and Sadducees here), didn't like Him. He brought to light some facts that some might prefer hidden. Jesus called these men a brood of vipers, which was accurate. But, some people will kill the messenger if they don't like the message.

Believers also have a responsibility to those around us, per Matthew 4:16, in that "the people living in darkness have seen a great light; on those living in the land of the shadow of death a light has dawned." While Jesus is the light, it's our job to "let your light shine before men that they may see your good deeds, and praise the Father in heaven" Matthew 5:16. You know, I can't repeat that verse without singing it, and that's how I typed it now, singing to the Donut Man tune.

Our Revelation quote is from 21: 23-24:  "The city does not need the sun or the moon to shine on it, for the glory of God gives it light, and the Lamb is its lamp.  The nations will walk by its light, and the kings of the earth will bring their splendor into it."  Now THAT's a BRIGHT LIGHT!

While there are far more quotes in Scripture about Jesus being light and the light of men, let me end with this thought from John 9:5 – "I am in the world, I am the light of the world."  As 1 Corinthians chapter 15 says, as pointed out above, Jesus has risen, and He is still in the world, so He is still the light of the world.
(July 2010)

# You Can't Have the Good Without the Bad

As a mommy I want to protect my children against every danger. This is normal. It's the precedent in nature. Every mommy elephant, deer, and badger will protect its babies from predators, enemies, and danger, even putting themselves in harm's way to save their offspring. Check out the nature channel if you want to see really inspiring scenes of familial love.

As a mother, as children grow, it's not enough to protect children from physical threats. We want to protect them from emotional threats, too. I want my children to be liked. I want other children and adults to be nice to my children. I want kindness to be the automatic response when my children are present. The truth is, that isn't how life works.

Just like you, I didn't have the perfect childhood. Other children were mean to me. Teachers sometimes took a dislike to me (albeit, I probably deserved it). Sometimes I did the right thing, but still lost. That's life. As a person, I can't change it for myself. And as a mommy, I can't change it for my children. So often, we wonder why the Lord doesn't interject something into our lives to stop the illnesses, job losses, challenges, and hurts from happening.

But, that wouldn't lead to growth.  A lot, and I mean the vast majority, of my growth came through the challenges.  When I was a little bit ahead in classes, mostly because I have a sister who is three years my senior who used to share her 6<sup>th</sup> grade knowledge with me when I was in 3<sup>rd</sup> grade, I was given the opportunity to learn ahead of my class.  I didn't always understand it, but at least I knew it was coming.  I remember learning the concept of negative numbers when I was in 5<sup>th</sup> grade, and I couldn't wait to get there in 8<sup>th</sup> grade math class!  But, when I did get there, and was ahead in math, I didn't experience a lot of growth.  In fact, I was probably at least a little bit contemptuous, because this was old information to me.  Like I said, I probably deserved it if teachers didn't like me.

Every one of us, if we can handle having to relive it, can think of a negative experience that lead to growth in us.  My youngest had probably the worst teacher who ever lived as his 3<sup>rd</sup> grade teacher.  I tried to get him out of her class, but the school didn't take well to that.  By the end of the year, my poor son hadn't learned much at all.  What happened was, as it was evident that the teacher had no tolerance for those students who forgot to put their names on their papers and other heinous infractions, the third grade students learned that they could be mean to these children without repercussion.  My son went from a friendly, well-adjusted child to a withdrawn little boy who lacks confidence.  Three years later, he still has a huge lack of confidence in academic matters.

But, this horrible experience has also made my son the most understanding and compassionate person.  So while I wish I could have better protected him, and that he had never endured what he did that year, amazing things will happen because of his experience.  That's Romans 8:28 at work—all things really do "work for the good for those who love the Lord and are called according to His purpose."  As a mommy, I'd like to ask why the Lord needed the endurance of an eight year old. I'll never know this side of heaven. The truth is that I don't know the Lord's plans, but I know that they're better than anything I can imagine. As horrible as it was to experience that year for both my son and me, we can already see the impact of the growth my son experienced that year.

So, as we end the Lenten season, and enter into the greatest joy of being a Christian, seeing Christ rise from the dead, we need to appreciate that the good couldn't have happened without the bad. It has been pointed out to me that God could have chosen another way of saving the world. But He didn't! The Lord, our Abba, the Father of our Lord Jesus Christ, who loved His son, and loves us, like babies, allowed His cherished child to, literally, go through h, e, double hockey sticks.

All four gospels record Jesus' giving up His spirit (Matthew 27:50, Mark 15:37, Luke 23:46, John 19:30). The man who knew no sin, who was perfect in every way, who never made a snide comment, never looked with less than love on everyone, even those who hated Him; the man who had the power to stop every act of evil against Him, instead chose obedience to the will of His Father, and in so doing fulfilled Old Testament prophecies. Jesus took everyone's sin and blame on Himself and descended into that most horrible place, in that He was absent from His father.

The Scriptures make it clear, this is something He didn't want to do. He asked that the cup be taken from Him, but even as He prayed that, He prayed that not His, but the Father's will, be done.

Do we do that? When we're going through the hard times—the financial challenges, the difficult bosses, the strained relationships—do we say, "Lord, you know I don't want to go through this, but not my will, Lord, but yours." Can we recognize that as we endure the tough times, we are being cleansed and dross is falling off us?

Can you see the difference in the way you respond to people now versus even a year ago?

The truth is, if we didn't have the challenges, the problems, the issues, the unfairness of life, we wouldn't be the people we are today.  Sometimes the Lord uses those challenges to make us run to Him. I promise, dear saints, that when we run to Him, He's running toward us, and will meet us more than halfway, with open arms, longing to surround us with His love and hold us tightly.

But, He may allow some bad times, just like He allowed Jesus to endure a horrible, painful death.  But, dear saints, the joy that is to come—maybe soon, maybe years from now, maybe in the next life—it will come! Whatever we're going through now, whatever our own black Friday may be, is nothing in terms of eternity.  As Jesus has His Easter celebration every year, we'll have our celebrations too.  We'll learn and grow and be better for the hard times. We'll be more understanding, more compassionate, more loving, more forgiving.  We'll think of others more and ourselves less.  We'll give more freely and laugh more loudly.  As we weather the storms, we'll see the rainbows.

(April 2009)

# Are you a Crier?

When we were little, didn't we laugh at criers? Even when my daughter was about four years old, and playing with the little boy across the street, who was a year older, when she started crying, this little boy immediately called her a cry baby. Even if he didn't raise his finger and point, I could see it in my mind. I'm sure it evoked memories of my childhood, and being called a cry baby.

Crying also suggests what I always heard of as being overly-sensitive. Oh, you're just oversensitive. Really? Maybe the fact that I just had my feelings hurt is legitimate? NO! You're just oversensitive. That gives all the people who make mean comments the right to hide behind the words, "it was a joke."

When I was in third grade—mind you, eight years old—our teacher, for reasons I can't fathom, chose to share with the class that a man was in a car accident. When they tried to call his wife, they couldn't find her (this was the 1960's, so cell phones wouldn't be around for decades), and later learned that she was also in the hospital. My little mind, and eyes, just wept for this unknown family. I raise my little hand and asked if we could pray for this family—I was in a private school, so that was acceptable. But, several of my classmates asked me afterwards why I had been crying. Why weren't they? How had eight year old hearts become so hardened that they hadn't cried to hear about this family? But what did I do? I lied. I told these children that I had something in my eye, so that I wouldn't be considered overly sensitive or, far worse, a cry baby.

Lately, I've noticed a lot of people are crying, me included. For years I've been aware that the easiest way to get me to bawl is to show me or tell me about tenderness. One story that still tears me up I heard years ago, about a plane going down over water, right at a riptide. The adults were strong enough to get past it, but the one little boy couldn't. The father realized his son couldn't make it alone, but that if he went after his son, he wouldn't have the energy to rescue them both. So he told his friends to tell his wife he loved her, and he swam to his son, and holding his baby, they both drowned. I'm tearing up just repeating the story! I'm a crier.

Wait, I have more. A few weeks ago at church we were having baptisms. After the pastor was done, a dad got in the water with his six year old daughter. She had to stand on the stool, because she was too short to sit on it. He asked her to give us her name, which she very quietly did. Oh, this sweet little princess totally had my heart! Praise the Lord for the humor she brought next, because it kept me from weeping openly. The dad asked, as he was supposed to, "have you accepted Jesus as your personal Savior?" And this sweet little Christian girl, whose name is written in the Book of Life, looked at her father and said, "Daaaaaaaaaad!" But even with the levity of the moment, seeing a daddy baptizing his daughter made me cry. It's just so sweet.

But it's not just me. Another week at church, our pastor was telling us, his congregation of thousands, that he loves us so much. And he got choked up just telling us this! An hour later, I heard a Sunday School teacher telling his class how much he loved them, and he got choked up. One day, when the pastor got to the end of the service and announced the altar call (this is where new believers are invited to come to the front of the church to make a quiet but public declaration of their salvation), an older gentleman sitting in a front row literally threw himself onto the steps. This church has eight steps that lead to the altar, and he crawled up those steps. A pastor went to him immediately to talk to him, and in leading him off to a private prayer room, the new Christian could barely walk. He was completely broken. It was a beautiful sight, and I cried like a baby. Is there anything more beautiful than seeing someone come to Christ?

So why are we suddenly seeing so many crying people? I've been in church for years and years, and having a pastor weep openly with the love he has for his congregation isn't the norm. Well, we have Scriptural support. First, from the Old Testament, Ecclesiastes 3:4 tells us there's "a time to weep and a time to laugh." It's good to know that the idea of balance is in the Bible. Yes, there's a time to weep. But, this too shall pass. And then there will be a time to laugh. And that, too, shall pass.

Psalm 30: 5 tells us that "weeping may remain for a night, but rejoicing comes in the morning." Again, the parallel is given. So even when the tears are tears of tenderness or joy, rejoicing and laughter follow.

Some of you may know the shortest verse in the Bible. John 11:35 – "Jesus wept." Two words. That's all. What was going on?

John 11 talks about the death of Lazarus. Lazarus, and his sisters Mary and Martha, were friends of Jesus. Because Lazarus was ill, the sisters sent word to Jesus. Jesus' response, in verse 4, was, "This sickness will not end in death. No, it is for God's glory so that God's Son may be glorified through it." Then, He stayed where He was for two more days.

What? You're told someone you love is sick, you know it is for God's glory that this is happening, yet you don't run? Okay. We'll just accept this. So, two days later, Jesus decides to return to Judea. His disciples reminded Him that not long before the people in that area had tried to stone Jesus. But Jesus assured them that Lazarus had fallen asleep and He was going to wake Lazarus. This wasn't clear to the disciples, but it would all be explained by the end of the chapter.

So upon arrival, happy to see Him, Martha verbally attacks him: "Lord, if you had been here, my brother would not have died." Well, hello to you too, Martha. I love Martha. I can so relate to her. Mary would say the same thing when she saw Jesus for the first time.

Now, this is where it gets really interesting. Verse 33 says, "When Jesus saw her (Mary) weeping, and the Jews who had come along with her also weeping, He was deeply moved in spirit and troubled." And then, two verses later, we read that Jesus wept.

Jesus wasn't weeping over Lazarus' death. It was seeing Mary and others weeping that moved Him to tears. It was tenderness. He couldn't stand seeing His precious friend in tears. And His tears did pass, and Lazarus' passing did result in glory for the Lord.

Maybe we need more tenderness in this world. Maybe it's okay to cry openly. Maybe things that make us cry are intended to bring glory to our heavenly Father, but we don't have the insight to realize it. In seeing a father baptize his daughter in Christ, I certainly was praising the Lord through my tears at the tenderness of the scene.

Maybe we need to stop thinking of criers as babies and instead see them as loving, caring, compassionate people. If you're not a crier, that's fine. I'm not encouraging anyone to begin crying, especially women, as it can make a complete mess of our make up, especially if we're wearing mascara. But opening our hearts, taking time to reflect on how we feel about others, using opportunities to express this love—what a better life we'll live, and what a better world we'll have; what a better legacy we'll leave behind, if we tuned in to that part of our hearts.

(May 2009)

# The Christian Life as a Piece of Furniture

Imagine a chair.  Imagine all the pieces that went into the chair.  For our purposes, imagine a soft, comfortable, cushy rocking chair.  Now, there are legs to that chair, that had to be fashioned.  There are springs in that chair, that had to be made, because metal springs don't grow in nature.  There is the soft, cushy, foam part of that chair—a seat to make our seat more comfortable.  And there is the outer shell, the material, that might be what attracted you to the chair in the first place.

Those legs had to be made.  Some older pieces, especially, had beautifully, intricately carved legs.  It might seem silly, because sometimes they were hard to see, but the intricacy and beauty are there.  We all had to be formed.

Now, the springs.  They are the nuts and bolts, along with nuts and bolts, of that chair.  They're what make the chair what it is. It's the underside that nobody sees that gives the chair the ability to hold person after person, year after year.  Without the nuts and bolts, the chair would fall apart. There's little glory to the springs— they're not pretty, they're not even seen.  But, sit on a bad spring, and you know it!  Sit on a quality chair with good springs, and you don't always appreciate it. But it's the inside of the chair that makes it quality.

The fluff of the chair. The padding. Some need more than others, because some are self-blessed with padding. The padding is good, but it's not the nuts and bolts. The padding is the feel good. Think of someone you know who makes people feel good. The touchy feely people out there are necessary, even if you're the nuts and bolts type. We can all add padding to our base and springs.

Now, the ornamentation. The pretty fabric in the pretty color. The perfect touch to the room. Yes, this is what attracts us to the chair, and to others, but it's not the real chair. Go sit on a chair without springs, nuts and bolts, and padding, and you'll find yourself on a piece of material on the floor, in what may be an undignified heap. The outward material is very important, it's what attracts us to the chair, but it's not enough alone.

As Christians, we are that chair. The base that holds us is Christ. Without the steady, strong piece, we've built our lives on nothing, and won't stand.

The nuts and bolts are our Bible study, prayer life, Christian fellowship, and daily walk with the Lord. It's where the real Christian life is put together. The better your springs, the better quality of chair you have. The craftsman who took a day and cheap parts to make a chair will have a cheap chair that won't last. But the craftsman who used good parts, and worked and reworked them, that's the quality chair we want to be. That's the craftsman who takes the chair apart every time he hears a squeak, to make sure all the parts are working. Nuts and bolts need to be tightened and adjusted and sometimes replaced. Keep up the Bible study, prayer time, fellowship, and church attendance.

The padding is hard for me. I'm a nuts and bolts girl. But, the padding is the feel good. It's the recognizing a new person at church, or the pat on the arm or arm around a shoulder while somebody is hurting. It's walking into a room and saying, "There you are!" and not, "Here I am." The padding is a very important part of the chair, but it's not enough alone. Imagine that padding over a poor quality chair. It will wear out faster and won't be used, because of the poor inside quality. But you do need that padding!

The material is the pretty façade. If it's all you have, it's nothing but a throw—an empty shell of material. But, pretty material over fluffy padding on top of quality building materials upon a beautifully carved base, that's something to see, and something to be. Start with the base. Be sure you're a new creation in Christ (2 Corinthians 5:17) Then, add the hardware. Pad it well. And finally, put on a beautiful cover of love and acceptance.

(March 2007)

# How Old Are You?

Oh, weren't we taught this is a naughty question? You don't ask people their age once they're into double digits, and you never, ever ask a lady her age—or has that era passed? Well, I hope so, because I'm here to ask you several of your ages.

First, you can think about your physical age if you choose. How many years ago were you born? Is this what you expected to feel like at this age? Is this what you thought life would be like? Are you happy with where you've landed? What disappointments do you need to face? What opportunities present themselves because of your age? No, I don't mean AARP.

Just this morning, a friend from College posted a comment that he can tell he's getting older. Aren't we all? With age, wrinkles, aches, and pains appear. But, some good things appear, too. One, I hope, is maturity. My maturity level may finally be approaching my chronological age. Two, knowledge. No matter how hard you try to avoid it, you're going to know more at 40 than you did at 20. Every experience will teach you something. Buy a house, and you're a font of information to someone untried in that area. Get and work a job, and you're a hero to someone who hasn't met that challenge yet.  Learn that we have two ears and one mouth for a reason, and know that this idiom is priceless to the young and/or foolish among us.

Second, let's think about our emotional age.  Are you mature?  Were you always more mature than your years?  Are you independent, interdependent, or dependent on others?  I was born old, but PTL I've become younger over the years.  I have a daughter who loves to take care of me, and while I hated that from friends and boyfriends and even my husband in my 20's and 30's, I relish it in my 40's.  I LIKE being taken care of, and being able to be emotionally young once in a while.  I'm not turning over all responsibility, but sometimes it's a nice break.

One of the nicest things about emotional age is that it can seesaw.  While chronological age is a steady increase, we can choose to be emotionally old one moment, and playing on the swing set the next.  It's fun to swing, and after a point, you stop worrying that others are watching and laughing at you on the swings.

Spiritually, how old are you?  You knew this is where we were going, didn't you?  When I first came to Christ, just shy of my 21st birthday, I was overwhelmed by what I didn't know.  It seemed everyone knew verses by heart, had something called Study Bibles—what are those?  Knew their books of the Bible in order so when the teacher asked us to turn, they could!  One time the guy sitting next to me gently whispered, "the other way," because I was flipping the wrong way in my Bible, looking for one book.  I was clueless!

With time, study, and effort, I've learned a lot.  I made up a song, first for the New Testament, then the Old Testament, to teach my children the books of the Bible in order.  At least my children could know that!  I'm not saying that this is the meat of Bible study, but it's nice to be able to find your way in this great book.

The point is, how mature are you spiritually?  When good times come, do you praise the Lord, knowing they are a gift from Him? I keep hearing about how people only pray when times are bad, and I'm not sure that's true. I do realize that it could be a sign of maturity. When good things happen, and you know to Praise the Lord, and not just accept it as though you are somehow deserving of good, that's maturity.

How about the bad times? Is this the only time you pray? Can you praise the Lord for the bad times, knowing that "all things work together for those who love the Lord and are called according to His purpose" (Romans 8:28)? Can you see past the bad times, knowing the Lord has something better planned for you (Jeremiah 29:11)? Can you praise the Lord during the bad times, knowing that this is an opportunity for you to grow and mature? Nobody wants bad times, but they can be great opportunities for us!

When I first started attending Bible studies, people kept turning to the mature women in the group. I LOVED being able to approach these incredible women for advice on marriage, children, friends, and family relationships. After about ten years, I found people turning to me. What? It seems my knowledge and learning had increased to the point where I was considered a mature Christian! I didn't accept it at first, and that's probably good. I haven't sat back believing I've reached maturity. I continue to study, memorize, learn, praise, and pray. None of us will reach the pinnacle this side of heaven, and that's okay. The question is, are you growing in your spiritual age? If not, why not? What can you do today, and tomorrow, and next week, and next month, to increase the number?

As I said, an interesting point is that two of the ages we discussed can increase and decrease. The physical age just keeps climbing, but emotional and spiritual ages can decrease as well as increase. Personally, I think it's a great idea to be emotionally young (but not immature), but spiritually mature.

# Praying Hard Prayers

Prayer is wonderful!  We're told to pray throughout Scripture, as found in 1 Thessalonians 5:17 – "Pray without ceasing." That's a verse short enough to be memorized.  The reference is almost longer than the verse!

But, some prayers are harder to pray than others. For instance, have you ever prayed for your children to be taken home?  Honestly, I have, but it took me almost a year after learning I should to honestly pray the prayer and mean it.

Have you ever prayed for unemployment?  While I haven't done that, once I found our family in unemployment, I praised the Lord loudly for it and could honestly say that I WANTED to be unemployed at that moment.

Have you ever prayed for a disease or illness?  Of course not, but can you see that when these horrible things happen great things can come from them? Romans 8:28 promises us:  "And we know that God causes all things to work together for good to those who love God, to those who are called according to His purpose."  Even diseases and illnesses.

Prayer is wonderful!  Some prayers are joyful to pray.  Praying that a relationship will lead to marriage, or for the health of an unborn child, are enjoyable prayers. We could pray those all day!  Some prayers are more pleas—for jobs, houses to sell, diseases and illnesses to be cured.  Some prayers are almost rote—our list of unsaved family members, prayers for leaders, traveling mercies.

But some prayers are tough.  Returning to the idea that people pray for their children to be taken home, I was originally shocked at this prayer, as you may be. And when I shared this prayer with a youth pastor at another Church, he told me he'd wished I hadn't told him.  This is the concept:  would you rather have your child taken from you before they reach the age of comprehension, and go to heaven, or have them with you in this world, but never come to a saving knowledge of Christ?  That's the prayer:  Lord, if my child is not going to come to a saving knowledge of Your Son, please take him/her home to heaven before they reach the age of understanding.

As I said, when I was told this with my first and, at the time, only child, who was about six months old, I was shocked.  I simply couldn't pray this prayer from my heart.  But, I decided to pray it in obedience, and after about a year, I truly meant it.  It took a year for me to mature to the point of wanting the best for my child— humans really are a sinful lot, aren't we?  So when I found I was expecting again, and then again, I was able to honestly pray this prayer, even while my boys were en utero.

Now I haven't exactly prayed for unemployment, but I can see where someone could.  I'm sure you've heard of examples of people being mistreated at work. Even at a new Bible study the other night, a woman shared that she hasn't been paid in a month.  She says she stays because the Lord hasn't told her to go yet. That's her decision, but if I were this woman, I'd be praying for a new job. Beyond that, I'd be praying to be fired so I could collect unemployment and have at least some income—more than she's getting now for working 40 hours a week.

In our situation, I've truly come to the point where I'm content to be unemployed. Yes, I memorized 1 Timothy 6:6, "But Godliness with contentment is great gain," during this season. I've learned that inside myself, I would rather be unemployed and in the Lord's will, than have a job and not be in the Lord's will. This concept can be parlayed into an innumerable number of other scenarios. While I wanted to have a baby years before I did, looking back, I'd rather be in the Lord's will to not have a baby than have a baby in my time, and not be in the Lord's will. The same is true with marriage. Better to be single in the Lord's will, than married and not married to the man the Lord chose for me, or married at the wrong time. Better to live in an apartment than buy a house out of the Lord's will. Better to attend College in the Lord's will, than somewhere I may want to go, not in the Lord's will. The options are endless for this prayer!

Logically, philosophically, rationally, intellectually, we understand this. But, and this is a huge BUT, emotionally, it's not always easy. While I can say I'd rather be childless if that's the Lord's will, I remember a lot of tears when it seemed that's what the Lord's will was for my life. And while I can praise the Lord loudly for our current unemployment, even while I'm in it, that doesn't mean there aren't some emotional times now.

When looking at 1 Thessalonians 5:17, it helps so much to look at the verses surrounding it: [16]"Rejoice evermore. [17]Pray without ceasing. [18]In everything give thanks: for this is the will of God in Christ Jesus concerning you."

These hard to pray prayers really need us to be rejoicing in the Lord first. Good prayer should start with praising, according to Scriptural models. I've even written on the ACTS prayer model—Adoration, Confession, Thanksgiving, and Supplication. Rejoicing comes first. After rejoicing and praising the Lord for our long list of blessings, pray without ceasing. I love the concept! If I spent my entire day in prayer, I wouldn't have time to yell at other drivers, or have a pity party for myself, or get annoyed with my children.

Then we're reminded to give thanks. We do have great blessings, especially when we live in the United States. And it's good to be reminded that wherever we are, this is God's will, in Christ, concerning us. God knows where we are. If it's time for you to pray the hard prayers, then do so. Pray in obedience, even the hard prayers.

(November 2009)

# Meeting the Kids

It's time for school to begin soon.  In Georgia, we're learning it starts very early—August 12th this year. The rest of the country probably has a few more weeks of summer vacation, but I'm hoping you can relate to this essay anyway.

Every day, at 2:30, 3:30, and 4:30, I will walk the quarter mile to the end of our street, to meet my children at the bus stop.  It's not that they can't walk the distance alone, it's that I want to meet them.  It gives me an extra seven minutes with them. Time after school, but before snack and homework.  Uninterrupted (for the most part) mommy/child time.  I live for that seven minutes every day.

One day last spring, while taking my quarter mile walk, I thought to myself, "My mother would find this ludicrous."  Why should I stop my projects, or whatever is keeping me occupied at the moment, for an extra seven minutes with my child?  I can't imagine my mother, or any of our neighbors growing up way back then, walking to meet my neighborhood friends or me. It simply wasn't done.

So why do I do it?  Originally, it was for the child's sake.  That first day of Kindergarten, when very little children get on very big buses, and drive away from home, without us. They haven't been without us for more than a few days, if ever, in their lives. And, now, to be driven away, for hours every day? Unthinkable. And they aren't going to the arms of loving grandparents, either. No, they're going to big, tall teachers who tower over them. The fact that these people are better trained in working with children than I am is irrelevant when it's my child in question. Remembering that thousands of children have similarly been ripped from their mommy's arms for scores of years softens the blow, when I could remember between sniffles and sobs.

But now, why do I do it? Why do I rush off the phone, leave dishes undone, leaves unraked, for more than the obvious—I didn't want to do those jobs anyway. Now, I do it for me. It's very selfish. I want to see my babies. I can't wait, even five more minutes, to hug my child.

Well, to put the Christian bent in here, if you can relate to what I'm saying, can you begin to understand how much God loves you? He runs to us! He can't stand having us away from Him for even a minute! He meets us at the bus, in the kitchen, while driving, even in the shower. (I love to pray in the shower—talk about focus.)

Yet, what did our Lord do? He sent His son, who, by the way, didn't want to go (Matt 26:39). My kids, by the way, were eager to go to school. It was mommy who had to get used to the idea. So the Lord sent His only child—let's stop again. You know, the first time I lead my daughter to the end of our driveway to wait for the bus (we had it easy back then), I still had two babies inside the house. I was sending my firstborn to school, but I still had two more toddlers inside to keep me busy and keep me from crying out loud, lest they wonder why mom was losing it. The Lord sent His ONLY child to the cross, and onward to hell, for three days. Now, I'm having a hard time with 3-6 hours of school. Despite what my sweet cherubs say, it's not H, E, double hockey sticks.

But, just as I go to meet my cherubs, the Lord comes to meet us.  God is waiting for us.  Every time we make a bad choice, or forget about Him for even a short while, He's there, waiting, and when we turn around and look for Him, HE RUNS TO US!  He misses us, just like we miss our babies while they're in school, and He can't wait even five more minutes for us to walk home.  He'll always meet you more than halfway.  And when we're together, oh what joy—like holding your babies in your arms!

(August 2007)

# Fall to be Lifted Up

WHAT A MODEL OF HUMILITY THE BIBLE GIVES US TO FOLLOW! I realize I yelled that statement, but it's so true! Look at Philippians 2:8 - "(Jesus,) being found in appearance as a man, He humbled Himself and became obedient to death—even death on a cross!"

The name that is above all names, the man who knew no sin, the only person who doesn't need to be punished, humbled Himself and died a sinner's death in a gruesome and horrible fashion. I'm not sure I could be that humble.

But let's back up before we go forward. Before we get to Philippians 2:8, we get to read Philippians 2:3-4 – "Do nothing out of selfish ambition or vain conceit, but in all humility consider others better than yourselves. Each of you should look not only to your own interests, but to the interests of others."

If we each did that, dear Saints, what a wonderful world this would be! What wonderful lives we would live! What wonderful witnesses we would bring! What a model of humility—to not do anything with the sole purpose of serving ourselves, but to consider others first, and look to others' interests. Wow. If I can do that for even an hour a day, I would live a better life.

Jesus confirms this message in Matthew 23:11, when He says, "The greatest among you will be your servant." Yes, we're told the greatest among us is the one who serves. That's so backwards to today's thinking. We're told we're great if others are serving us, but His ways are not our ways. Again, we're told to look to the interests of others, while the world tells us to look out for number one.

So what is the result of humbling ourselves for the sake of others? The Bible covers that more than once. In Matthew 23:12, Jesus tells us, "For whomever exalts himself will be humbled, and whomever humbles himself will be exalted." Luke records the same thought in 18:14. Let's think about this. If we humble ourselves, the Lord will exalt us. That's reason enough right there to obey!

This thought is again repeated in James 4:6 – "God is opposed to the proud, but gives grace to the humble." And again in James 4:10 – "humble yourselves in the presence of the Lord, and He will exalt you at the proper time." And in Luke 1:52b – [He] has exalted those who were humble."

1 Peter 5:6 says, "Therefore, humble yourselves under the mighty hand of God, that He may exalt you at the proper time."

Have you ever overheard someone saying something nice about you? Sometimes they say it right in front of you, "Well, if you want to play a real competitor, you should play against Chris here. Talk about someone good!" Doesn't it make you feel great—and possibly surprise you? It's wonderful to hear compliments like this.

But what about when we compliment ourselves? "Well, to be honest, I'm really the best one at that." It may be true, but it rings hollow in our own ears. We're taught to not be conceited or egotistical, right? Well, that idea probably came from the Bible, because ego and pride are often synonymous. The point is, when you humble yourself, it's the Lord who will exalt you. Now, I love a compliment as much as anyone, but to hear it from the Lord!

I have to wonder, how will we receive these blessings? First, it tells us, we'll have grace. I could certainly use more of that! Second, we will be exalted. I have to wonder then, how will the Lord exalt us? For one, it may be an assignment, which doesn't sound like much of an exaltation. But, there are jobs we would love to have. Would any of us turn down the job of President? Probably not. So the Lord may choose to exalt you with a job or assignment, or maybe with honoring children. That would be a truly miraculous and wonderful way to be exalted. I'm just thinking out of the box here. What way would you like to be exalted this side of heaven? Or, He may wait until heaven to exalt you. Either way, the point is that since He's promised to do it, you know He will!

So humble yourself—admit you can't do it without Him, ask for assistance, call upon the Spirit's strength—and wait to be lifted up.

(November 2010)

# Camping Out or Moving In?

In today's world, I'm guessing very few, if any, of us have never been through a move.  My husband and I, no lie, have moved fifteen times in our marriage.  Most of these moves were early in our marriage and due to job changes.  Our last move, due to a job change, was three years ago, and nothing in my life had prepared me for that move.

First, we were moving ourselves.  Second, we had three children.  Third, we had lived in that house for over ten years.  Imagine how many things can accumulate when you raise three children over a ten year span in one place.  We saw toys, furniture, and appliances come and go during that period.  Okay, mostly come and stay.

The five hundred mile move taught me a great deal.  We had sold a lot of furniture, but moving to an area as expensive as Atlanta, our house is much smaller and a lot just didn't fit, or didn't have a place.  You can only plan to a certain extent.  Further, for the first time in ten years, I had to think every time I went out.  I could get to the kids' school, and I could get to the grocery store, but getting from the kids' school to the grocery store took some major concentration.

But, this was our new home. I was determined to learn all I could about the area and make our house into a home. So I got busy creating a home. We bought furniture and finally began using our once-empty family room. I spent an entire morning figuring out what cabinets best fit cereal boxes and what shelves in the pantry could handle two cans of stacked soup. We unpacked books and decorations and moved furniture in circles until we found what worked best. We learned what was better about this house, what we missed about the last one, and how to make accommodations.

Now, please know that I'm married to an Eagle Scout. Please know that I don't camp. Right after our move, our youngest decided to join Boy Scouts, taking his older brother on his journey. Suddenly, we were awash in uniforms, tents, and camping equipment. Camping equipment is fascinating. While items for my house are supposed to be functional and decorative, camping equipment has two goals—functional and light. That's it. Does it work, and is it light enough to carry any distance?

What a difference! While I'm creating an abode, my family is collecting things to be used temporarily. Ah, I see a great Scriptural correlation here: Exodus 19:2 – "After they set out from Rephidim, they entered the Desert of Sinai, and Israel camped there in the desert in front of the mountain."

Camping suggests a temporary living situation—a temporary, impermanent, shelter called a tent; Lightweight plastic implements that can often be tossed when used; Small, lightweight appliances to be carried. I mean, I have a stove! It weighs far too much to be taken backpacking or even camping (there is a difference, I learned), but it cooks and bakes and simmers and anything else I need to do when cooking or baking. And it's still there tomorrow, and with the flick of a wrist, I get heat.

It doesn't work that way with camping. Camping is a temporary situation—for a night or two, a week at the most. We bring what we need, and take it all with us when we leave. You've heard the admonition—take only pictures, leave only footprints. That's camping.

So, in our Christian walk, are we moving in or camping out? Do you want to come into the body of Christ, stay for a short while, and then pick up and move on? Do you want to hang out for a few days or nights at the most, see what it's all about, and then move on to your next destination? I hope not!

When you come to Christ, the goal is that as He dwells in your heart, you start to look like Him. You come to Him so completely, with your mind, mouth, and heart, that you move in completely. You redecorate your home with Christian art. Your bookshelves now reflect the new man you are in Christ (2 Corinthians 5:17). Your shopping habits may even change—where once you bought cigarettes and alcohol, you may be purchasing more fruit and veggies, because your body is a temple (1 Corinthians 6:19).

Your time is spent differently. You no longer spend Sunday morning at the Church of the Mattress, as I once heard it called by a student. Your Wednesday nights are full! You get up early to spend time in prayer and study. Weekends that were once filled with parties are now filled with something called fellowship—still parties, but with a common purpose. Every discussion isn't about Christ and Salvation, but He's there for every conversation.

Work is suddenly better, because you're seeing the big picture. Galatians 6:9 says, "And let us not be weary in well doing: for in due season we shall reap, if we do not grow faint," and it suddenly makes sense! Family and friend relationships are improving, because you're doing "all things without complaining or arguing" (Philippians 2:14), and having "nothing to do with stupid and petty arguments" (2 Timothy 2:23). You're really caring about others, and listening to others, and wanting what's best for them, and they sense it in you, and respond to it.

Do you see, can you appreciate, the difference between moving in and camping out? One is long-term, one is short term. One uses substantial furniture and appliances, one uses foldable furniture and gadgets that can be carried and stowed. One will lead you to eternal life, the other to eternal damnation. One will give you a forever friend who will see you through every joy and challenge, one will leave you bereft and alone.

Come on, dear Saints. Build your house on the rock and move into a mansion with thousands like me. Don't just camp out.

(October 2009)

# An Angel's Tale

The young angel knew he was ready for his wings. With determination he approached his father.

"You do know what is required for angels like us to earn our wings," said his father. The young angel wasn't sure if it was a question or a statement, but nodded his understanding.

There were lots of different kinds of angels in heaven, and they all earned their wings different ways. It seemed to him his were the hardest to earn, but he was ready. He was a Memory Angel, as were his parents. Whenever a mortal was feeling bad or having a hard time, memory angels reminded them of nice things that had happened to them. Some of the memories were easy to invoke, like a new baby or a wedding. But the most useful memories were nice things that had happened for no obvious reason--someone had done something nice, a random act of kindness. This is what lead to the requirement for Memory Angels to earn their wings.

A Memory Angel had to find a mortal doing a simple act of kindness. The young angel's father said it was easier years before, when he had earned his wings as a young angel. But it seemed that simple acts of kindness were more rare today. But the young angel knew he was ready, and he knew it even more strongly whenever he heard a bell ring. Everyone knew that every time a bell rings an angel gets their wings.

Looking at his son's determined face, the father said, "If you're sure, son, I'll take you down to earth, and we'll look for some simple acts of kindness. Do you know where you want to look?"

Oh, the little angel was all ready for this question. He had thought a lot about what kind of people would do nice things for no reason, and he just knew he needed to go where all the rich people were. So at his request the two angels set off for a very fancy benefit in one of the biggest cities on the earth, the father carrying the wingless son.

The little angel's eyes almost popped when he arrived. The room was very glittery, with lots of gold lamps and candles, even though it was very bright. The male mortals all wore fancy clothes his father called tuxedoes and the female mortals wore dresses of the brightest colors. All around their hands and faces they wore shiny stones. The young angel assumed they were trying to look like cherubim with all that glittery stuff, but he knew cherubim's glow was from an inner radiance. All the people talked a lot about how much money they give to poor people, so the young angel knew he had come to the right place.

When a female mortal slipped, causing a tearing sound from her dress, the young angel was ready to watch someone offer assistance, but nobody came forward and the embarrassed mortal left as quickly as she could. When an older mortal spoke of how much money he gave, others around him smirked. This wasn't kindness at all.

The father saw the sad look cross his son's face and took him out of the room. "Well, shall we return to heaven now?" he asked. But the young angel wasn't ready to admit defeat. He had more than one idea of where to find kindness. If rich mortals weren't being kind, surely the very strong were kind.

The young angel immediately found himself at a quarry--that's what his father said it was. There were many male mortals, all trying to break large rocks with picks and axes. Some of the mortals were tall and strong with big shoulders. They broke their rocks easily. Others were different heights and some were very young and obviously not as strong. The young angel grinned at his father and said, "We only have to wait," and sat down with a smile. But after much waiting, he saw that nobody was helping the younger and weaker mortals. In fact, they were totally ignored. He was sure one of the strong mortals would show compassion, but after a long while, even in angel-time, the young angel had to admit that he would not see any random acts of kindness here.

The young angel felt totally dejected. The father watched his son's face closely. He watched as his son's look of confidence changed to concern, then to surprise, and finally defeat. Just before the tears came, a sign of defeat for an angel, the father spoke.

"Well, where would you like to go now?"

"I guess it's not time for my wings yet. I guess we should just return home, but," and his voice caught a little as he finished, "you'll have to carry me again."

"Why don't we try one more place, son?" said the father, as he lifted the young angel onto his shoulders. And as he was the one flying, the son had no alternative but to go along.

The young angel found himself in a small town on a sunny and warm day. There were many mortals around, males and females of all ages. None seemed especially rich, and none appeared especially strong. In fact, everybody appeared rather ordinary. There were grown mortals with miniature mortals, going in and out of stores. There was a group of female mortals sitting on benches, each with at least one miniature mortal occasionally running to them to say or ask something.

One of the miniatures must have very recently been brought by the Birth Angel, for it was as small as he'd ever seen one in heaven.  The few times he had snuck into the Birth Angel's area he saw that all mortals were tiny.  It wasn't until his father had shown him the earth a few aeons before that he learned they only start out that way.

All in all, it wasn't a very inspiring scene for the young angel.  What good could possibly be done here?  Even as he glumly watched, thinking this entire trip to have been a huge waste of time, he watched an older female mortal come out of a store.  She was carrying two brown bags overflowing with food--something his father informed him mortals needed to continue on earth.

The young angel looked past her and saw a group of young mortal males playing a game.  Baseball he knew and he watched as the batter hit a foul ball and one of the other male youths race after it, bringing him closer.  The boy was as typical as anything else the young angel was observing today—medium height and build, curly hair that he was trying to hide under a baseball cap, buck teeth.  An ordinary young mortal, and with his limited research, of no particular interest to a young angel trying to earn his wings by observing a random act of kindness.

A beep from a car horn caught his, and everyone else's, attention.  The elderly female mortal, with two bags of groceries obscuring her vision, had inadvertently walked too far into the street and was pushed back by the horn.  In reversing direction she stumbled and fell, and her groceries ran all over the sidewalk.

Then something he didn't expect to happen occurred right before his eyes.  The young mortal threw the ball back to the game and signaled for them to continue playing without him.  There was some urging for him to continue playing, whether because he had thrown the ball well or because he was needed to continue play was unclear to the young angel.  Ignoring the calls from the other mortals, the youth started gathering the groceries that lay scattered near him. After catching a few rolling objects he helped the female mortal to her feet before gathering the rest.

The young angel approached the two so he could hear their conversation.

"You look a bit shaky, ma'am," the youth was saying. "I'll carry this bag, and you better hang on to me while we cross the street."

The older mortal seemed surprised but pleased by the youth's gallantry, but as they stepped into the street her surprise turned to appreciation for she was a bit shaky. The female had informed the youth that her home was a few blocks away. Her husband normally drove her the short distance, but he wasn't feeling well, and with the nice weather she thought she would enjoy the walk, especially because she didn't think she was buying that much. At this both mortals grinned, since each was carrying a full bag, all the bulkier as they had been repacked in the street by an inexperienced youth.

As they neared the female's home the angel saw her digging in what she called her purse before she informed the youth, "It seems I've left my keys. Would you be so kind as to ask my husband to let us in?"

The young angel had enjoyed the scene—in fact it somehow made him feel good, although why he wasn't sure. He turned to his father ready to ask for a ride back to heaven. His father was looking at him funny—kind of like he knew something that the young angel didn't. He puzzled over it for a minute, then shrugged, when in the back of his mind, he heard it. He quickly turned and saw the young mortal ringing the doorbell. Together, the two angels flew home.

(December 2007)

# Prayer Time

Hello again. Now that autumn is definitely on its way, and routines are returning or kicking in, I thought it might be time to refresh ourselves with prayer. To that end (I really talk that way), I thought we would review an outline you may have been taught for praying. I didn't learn this until I had children, and I've taught this to my children. My preference is ACTS, because I learned it first, and it's easy for me to remember. But, PCTI is the exact same order.

ACTS stands for Adoration, Confession, Thanksgiving, and Supplication. PCTI stands for Praise (adoration), Confession, Thanksgiving, and Intercession (supplication). In my children's cases, I just told them they could ask for what they wanted at the end, until they were old enough to understand the words supplication and intercession.

The first word, Adoration, is a lovely thought. We adore our God; we adore His son; we adore the Holy Spirit. So when we are praying, to whom do we direct our prayers? Well, a good way to start is with the names of God. When I am praying for support, I might call on my Abba, my Daddy. Sometimes, I just need to crawl into His lap and tell Him about my day. When stressed, I might pray to Jehova Shalom, the God of Peace.  I seem to live with angst on a daily basis, and I often need the comforting hand of Jehova Shalom, so if I come to the Father in adoration with this name, my prayers are all set up.

Confession is good for the soul, right?  Well, let's look at confession.  Confession can be as public or private as you choose.  Saying you're sorry to God is a great place to start.  Just admitting your error finds favor with God.  But, it doesn't have to stop there.  Admitting your transgression to your friend/spouse/neighbor/child really does honor the Lord.

Thanksgiving should be easy, but daily?  Hourly?  Come on! 1 Thessalonians 5:17-18 tells us to PRAY CONTINUALLY, GIVING THANKS IN ALL CIRCUMSTANCES.   The continually after the word pray, means all the time.  Every minute. Some people have this down to a science, and can make every breath a prayer; or can carry on a conversation, all the while offering up prayer.  I've known some to set timers to remind them to keep prayer as part of their daily life.  And the giving thanks in ALL circumstances means you don't get to pick and choose.

I remember when I was first taught this concept in College.  I looked at the Pastor like he had two heads.  And, sassy as I was (am), I had the nerve to say something about having multiple tests, work, and roommate problems.  And he smiled in his Scriptural wisdom and assured me that God already knew my schedule.  And what a wonderful beginning of my spiritual growth, as I learned to praise and thank the Lord, even in the hard times.  That's a prayer that honors the Lord, and the Lord can honor.

Now, supplication is a great word.  The first verse I ever memorized was Philippians 4:6 (although I couldn't give you the address for years):  "Be anxious about nothing, but in all things, with prayer and supplication, with thanksgiving, present your requests to

the Lord." So here we are, being told the whole of
prayer in one verse. Don't worry, just pray and ask. But
don't forget the thanksgiving (see paragraph above).
We're also told we have not because we ask not. Here,
we're told to ask. I've been told to be obedient. Okay! I
can obey this part. I won't worry, and I will ask for
wisdom, guidance, and help. I don't think it's any
accident that we ask last, after adoring, confessing, and
thanking the Lord.

A few other thoughts on prayer. First, when do
we pray? According to Mark 1:3-5, in the morning.
Mark 6:46-47 tells us in the evening. Luke 6:12 tells us
to pray all night. So, I'm guessing it's a personal matter.
Until we learn to pray continually, pray when it works
best for you. I've admitted before, my favorite times to
pray are in the shower and the car. The shower usually
starts my day off well, but back in my single days, when
I would take a second shower for a date, I would find
myself automatically praying. What a blessing that was!
Driving is something I find myself doing alone more often
as the children grow. It's a lovely time to find myself
alone with the Lord, and we can have some great
conversations. You can always turn up the music, roll up
the windows, and sing to the Lord. He'll hear you, but
nobody else will. I can't sing when others are in the
house. Even as a young child, my son would put his
hands over my mouth if ever I sang. I got the point.

Continuing the question of when to pray, it's more
than just the time of day. According to James 1:5-6,
pray when making a decision. 1 John 1:9 tells us to pray
after sinning.

2 Corinthians 1:3-4 tells us to pray for comfort.
Ephesians covers all the bases by telling us in 6:18 to
pray for all occasions. I think it brings credence and
humility to the prayer when you match your prayer to a
Bible verse. I try to start group prayer with Matthew
18:20,"Where two or more are gathered, God is there."
That's a positive way to begin.

Okay, to finish, why do we pray?  Beyond the above reasons, to adore our Lord, offer confession and give thanks, and simply make requests, Scripture offers some specific reasons.  Psalm 90:12 tells us we pray to learn.  Psalm 50:15 and John 15:8 echo each other while the first tells us our prayer pleases God, and the second tells us our prayers help us know God.  Psalm 8:2 tells us our prayer will help us know His will.

Adding a little prayer to your life can truly help you walk closer to the Lord's will. It keeps you in touch with the Lord during the day, which could lead to less stress, and a happier life.
(September 2009)

# Forgiveness

There's a lot of ugliness in today's world. A LOT of it! There's ugliness on a world-wide scale with terrorism and people hating you, and me, just because we live in the United States. Talk about bigotry on a whole new level—geographic hatred. Think about that. Somebody hates you, and your family and neighbors, because you're American. It's not enough that ugliness was already dictated by race and gender, but now geographically.

But there's ugliness in the United States too. We're in an election year, and on a daily basis I hear the most absurd statements based on people's independent thoughts and choices. Praise the Lord we live in a country that allows us to speak in the street, at work, or even on the radio and say what we think and believe, no matter how absurd or ugly it is.

It gets worse. There's ugliness at work. It doesn't matter where you work, or how far from home, or what you do. There is stress and ugliness from any number of sectors—bosses, underlings, counterparts. And it's not necessarily personal. Somebody had a bad night, possibly through no fault of their own, so their mood affects them which affects you so now you're in a bad mood—and you didn't do anything wrong. In fact, you did everything right, but you're still having an ugly day.

And then there's home. Our castles, right? Mine is far less than a castle, although I'm more than content with the generous lot the Lord provides for us. But, even within the confines of my own home, we have marital ugliness, parental ugliness—I am learning a whole new level of ugliness from children as they reach the teen years. I mean ugly behavior to each other, and ugly behavior to me—and I'm the mommy! This isn't supposed to happen.

Ah, but it is. It is promised in the Bible. We will have problem when we choose that rocky road. But I'd rather be on this road to salvation than the easy road to hay, wouldn't you?

So based on the title above, you know what I'm about to say here. Forgiveness needs to be a decision when we get up in the morning; that we pray through all day long; and our decision before the ugliness ever hits.

Matthew 18:35 says, in the NIV, "This is how my heavenly Father will treat each of you unless you forgive your brother from you heart." Wow, that sounds more like a threat than a promise. There is much to be said in Scripture on forgiveness, including, of course, Jesus' plea from the cross for the Lord to forgive those who crucified Him, even in His pain. That's forgiveness!

I have a favorite quote on forgiveness, that you may know, that I heard once and have remembered to this day: Forgiveness is the fragrance left by the flower on the sole of the boot that crushed it. Isn't that poetic? I really think it's beautiful, and I'm not that into poetry. But it's memorable. Can you be a fragrance for someone today?

A fragrance can arrive before you, and linger after you're gone. Fragrances and aromas can arouse great desire, even physical hunger, in us. They can bring both happy and painful memories. Of our five senses, smell is possibly the most ignored or taken for granted, but they say 90% of our taste comes from the smell, so there must be something to it. Think what an impact forgiveness could have after you've left, or before you arrive the next time.

Back to Matthew 18:35. The reason I want to stop at this verse is to point out the end—"from your heart." Now, it helps if you know that in Jesus' day, it was commonly believed that different parts of our bodies held different aspects of our being. Please allow me to explain. It was believed that the kidneys held our emotions and our conscience. The legs held our character. There are too many jokes and comments to be made for that one, and out of fear that I'll digress, I choose to pass. The stomach held heartfelt emotions and desires. Really. I'm not making this up! And the heart, our heart, is our source of intelligence.

Now, this is a whole new concept to me. Forgiveness is simply the intelligent decision. Not the kind, merciful, Christian decision. It's simply smart. Let's think about all of this. First, it is the kind decision. When somebody cuts you off in traffic, choose ahead of time to forgive them. You'll be the kind driver. The next time a spouse or child gets sassy or ugly, be merciful and forgive them. The Lord will treat you the same the next time it's your error. It is the Christian decision, as we see again when Jesus died on that cross and chose to forgive, and prayed to His Father to forgive, even in His pain. Those are three legitimate reasons to forgive.

But the intelligent decision. This is brilliant, no pun intended. When you forgive others, you create a debt. You could hold the grudge, which by the way, will be far heavier for you to carry than the other person, anyway. But you could. If/when you are legitimately wronged, a debt is created. By choosing to forgive the debt, you create goodwill. (Yea, we're back to creating, my March article.) Anyway, you do create good will, and you create, in our American Society, a reciprocity agreement, even unstated.  In the United States, and other places I'm sure, but my research only supports the U.S., we don't accept favors graciously all the time.  In fact, we'll turn away favors rather than owe somebody something.  But nobody can refuse forgiveness, because it's not their decision, it's ours.  So when you forgive others, it leads them to forgive you in future, or maybe others.  Maybe somebody you don't know and will never meet.  Maybe it's a long term quarrel, and through your forgiveness of one person, they'll in turn follow your example and forgive others, and a rift of long-tenure will be healed.  Of course we can't know this, but the Lord does.  And He sees us.  And He's smiling.  He really does love us, doesn't He?  And He's forgiven us more than we can ever forgive anybody else.

So let's make a decision on a daily basis to practice forgiveness for maybe even one day.  If the mail is late, the check doesn't come, people are rude, sales clerks are busy talking rather than working—let's make a decision to forgive before it ever happens.  We'll probably be happier at the end of the day, too, just as a bonus.  Wouldn't that be lovely?

I do love and pray for you dear, dear saints.
(July 2008)

# What To Do When
# You Don't Know What To Do

One of the interesting things about this job is that I really don't feel like I write these articles. Everything I've written has been directed by the Lord—not that I'm claiming this is God-breathed stuff. Not at all! But I get ideas for articles in different settings and situations, and the Lord nudges me when He wants me to write on a specific topic.

I've had the notes for today's articles for a while and felt the Lord was telling me to write this article for April. Well, I'm definitely the kind of girl who doesn't do what I want to do, until I do what I have to do—it's a rule in our home. So while I planned and hoped to spend yesterday researching and writing, the day got filled in with a lot of to-do's. It was a successful day, but I never got to touch the article.

This morning I had kind of an ugly start. One son left his homework out, and when I looked it over, I found some glaring errors, such as page three being stapled into the pack upside down. Being a teacher, this kind of oversight really bothers me. Then I learned another child wasn't completing homework, which again as a teacher, confuzzles me. How do you not turn in homework? It goes against my grain.

So when I pulled out the topic and the notes I'd taken, I'm humbly amazed at what the Lord is teaching me today. When it comes to being a mommy, a job I've only had for 15 years, and received with very little training, I constantly find myself in a position of having to do something when I don't know what to do. Sometimes it's very specific, like when the note comes home from the teacher, and a decision has to be made—do we offer mercy or punishment?

But I had thought about this article from a higher plane, like when major things go wrong, or a major catastrophe hits, what to do. But I realize, very humbly I assure you, that the truths in God's word are as true and as needed in the daily and small challenges, maybe more, as they are in life's more obvious obstacles.

Let's start with Psalm 128:1 (NIV) – "Blessed are all who fear the Lord, who walk in His ways."

So we are first told to fear the Lord. Many of you might know that the word fear, in the Old Testament, best translates as Respect. So, first and foremost, when you find yourself in a situation where you don't know what to do, remember to first respect the Lord.

How to show respect? I'm sure you can think of several ways with me. Let's use our senses. First, look at the person whom you want to respect. While the preacher is speaking on Sunday morning, watch him—keep your eyes on him as he speaks. If you're looking around the sanctuary you could be distracted from the teaching. In a conversation with another person, of course you maintain eye contact to show you're interested and listening to what the other person is saying, and you expect the same from others. So, first, keep your eye on the Lord.

Second, listen. That doesn't sound hard, because our ears are working 24/7, even when we're asleep. That's why the alarm works. But we all know that hearing and listening aren't the same thing. Truly listen to what the Lord is trying to say to you. It's probably easiest to hear Him if you're not preoccupied and doing several things at a time.

I know in our culture, multi-tasking is not only expected, but it's required. If it weren't for washing machines and dishwashers, I couldn't get all my housework done in a day—and for one wonderful day have a clean house. My! But I digress. While multi-tasking can be a good thing, when showing respect, stop it. Sit and listen to what the other person is saying. You'll find the Lord has a lot to say to you, personally, when you are listening, and not just hearing. I learned the importance of showing respect this way from someone near and dear to me, my oldest son. From a very young age, when my son needed to talk to me about something, it was never enough for me to chat while I made supper. No. He needed me to sit across the table from him and look him in the eye, to prove I was listening. It's still true of him more than my other two today, but it's a good lesson for all of us.

Psalm 34:8 tells us to "taste and see the goodness of the Lord," right? But that's only the first half. The second half tells us, "blessed is the man who takes refuge in Him." There is happiness and joy, there is blessing, in tasting the Lord's goodness—in taking refuge in the Lord. So the next time you don't know what to do, taste the Lord's goodness with your ears and eyes, and take refuge in Him!

Okay, specifically, how? Pray as Jesus prayed. Never did Jesus set out on His own. Even though He and the Father were one, He spent hours and hours in prayer. If you don't think you have time to sit and pray, then stand and pray. Pray in the shower; pray while you make breakfast; pray in line—we all spend lots of time in lines! If we could harness that time into useful prayer time, we could change the world!

Another way to take refuge in the Lord? Praise Him! You have to feel closer, and more intimate, with the Lord when you're telling Him how wonderful He is! Name some of His attributes—Counselor, Mighty God, Healer, Provider—whatever works for you today. And don't just think it. Say it! Praise Him out loud and loudly. Shout out in the shower, "Lord, You are fabulous! This is the day You created, I will rejoice and be glad in it! I will rejoice and be glad in You, for I am wonderfully made." Okay, I snuck two verses into that one, but you can shout anything you want. Be loud and be proud, and you'll get your direction of what to do when you don't know what to do.

Keep your Bible handy. I started in a new office in January, and it was just this past week I took a Bible to leave in my office. I got tired of carrying books back and forth, so I brought a Bible with me to keep in the office, so it's always convenient and readily available. Next, pick it up. Even holding His Word will make you feel closer to the Lord. Even better, read it. It doesn't matter where you start, but if you've never read the Bible for the pure joy of it, I always suggest starting in the gospels. It's the greatest story, but I'll warn you, what's written doesn't include the end, and that could bother some readers. We do know the end of the story, but it hasn't been written yet. In the meantime, it's a good story to know.

The last thing I have to share is quite basic. If you haven't yet asked Jesus to be Lord of your life, if you've never prayed the ABC prayer, or the sinner's prayer, or the Roman Road, take the time now to do so. The ABC prayer says: ADMIT you're a sinner; BELIEVE Jesus died on that cross for you, personally; and COMMIT your heart and life to Him. Ask Jesus to live in your heart. It's the best decision you'll ever make. The sinner's prayer and Roman Road both start with Romans 3:23— "For all have sinned and fall short of the glory of God."

That's right, we're all sinners, and there's no degree of sin in the Bible. So if you think your sins are somehow worse than others, or that God could never forgive your sins, get over yourself. We're all sinners, from Adam and Eve down to you and me. We're it, baby. We are the reason Jesus came and we celebrate Easter. Of course, the sin part is the ugly part. The beauty is that Jesus did come and offers the gift of salvation (Romans 5:8) to anyone who merely asks.

If you don't know what to do, whether it's a small challenge or a major life decision, give it over to Jesus. Turn to God, pray and praise, study the Bible, and put yourself on the path of righteousness. God is waiting for you to cast all your cares upon Him, for He cares for you (1 Peter 5:7).

(April 2008)

# LOL

If you're clued into the real world, you're well aware of the shorthand used to text.  You would therefore know that LOL means Laugh Out Loud.  I have another meaning for LOL and why it's in the order it is.

I think LOL means Listen, Obey, and Learn.  From our earliest years, we are taught to listen.  If we obey, we are rewarded—with knowledge, with approval, sometimes even with a cookie or some other treat.  It was true when we obeyed our parents, our teachers, our Pastors, even our friends.  And in so doing, we learn.  We learn our numbers, our letters, history, math, and we learn the importance of obedience so we can learn.

So how do we listen to the Lord?  I think, first, with our heart.  We know right from wrong and good from bad. Of course, being in the word daily is a great starting place, because amazing nuggets of truth are there, but it's not enough to just read them, we have to listen to them.  But the Lord often sends messages other ways.  For instance, I remember a time years ago, every time I opened my Bible, went to church, or attended a Bible study, it seemed the same message kept coming out over and over.  I think the Lord was trying to get my attention.  Or it could be with a friend.  Has someone

ever told you something that was so obvious to them,
but was amazingly insightful to you? That could be the
Lord talking through someone.

Back to LOL, how often do we want to rearrange
these? Remember it's listen, obey, then learn. But how
often are you asked, especially by children, "why?"
We're trying to put the learn before the obey. We hear
the call, even something as simple as, "Please come
here." The appropriate response would be to obey, and
go. But instead we query, "Why?"

Well, let's see some Biblical answers why
obedience should come immediately. Maybe, in that
way, we can be quicker to keep it LOL instead of LLO.

First, Jesus tells us, in Luke 11:28, "Blessed are
those who hear the word of God and obey it." He doesn't
tell us we're blessed if we hear it, think about, discuss it
with friends, weigh the advantages and disadvantages,
and then choose to obey it. We hear and obey—quickly,
immediately, and without question. If we do that, what
happens? WE ARE BLESSED! There's a great reason
right there to obey what we hear.

But, we don't know what we'll be asked to do,
right? Well, the Bible has some amazing examples for us
to follow. In Hebrews 11:8, the great faith chapter of
the Bible, we're reminded about Abraham: "By faith
Abraham, when called to go to a place he would later
receive as his inheritance, obeyed and went, even
though he did not know where he was going." Abraham
didn't know he was going to receive this land as his
inheritance, and in fact, he didn't even know where he
was going! In today's world of mapquest, that just
doesn't work for us. I have a huge fear of maps and
unknown places—kind of amazing that I work as a
speaker going unknown places, by the way—but we're
told to GO. In obedience. Abraham did it. Others do it.
Be obedient, and go when called.

And let's look at Jonah. You know, I never read
the book of Jonah until I was an adult. I knew the story

as a child, but it wasn't until I had known Jesus as my personal Savior for years that I read these four short chapters. My, what a surprise! Jonah was not always the nice guy I saw in my childhood storybooks. But, in chapter 3, verse 3, it does tell us that, "Jonah obeyed the word of the Lord and went to Nineveh." But, if you look two verses above, you'll see firsthand that God is the God of second chances: "Then the word of the Lord came to Jonah a second time." Yes, Jonah obeyed, but it took him two chances to get it right.

Isn't that encouraging? If there's something you've been called to do, you still have time. Write that symphony, call your friend, share the gospel with a brother—whatever it is, you get another chance—you still have time. Personally, there have been times I've needed more than two chances to obey, but the Lord keeps our transgressions as far as the east is from the west (Psalm 103:12). The important thing is to obey now.

The Bible offers another great reason to be obedient in Romans 6:16, which says, "Don't you know that when you offer yourselves to someone to obey him as slaves, you are slaves to the one whom you obey— whether you are slaves to sin, which leads to death, or to obedience, which leads to righteousness." Now, does anyone intentionally want to be slaves of sin, which leads to death? Of course not! But one of the blessings of obedience is that it leads to righteousness. I memorized a definition of righteousness years ago when I was reading a Bible dictionary (yes, I'm a nerd). It simply said, "turning toward God." I love that! The righteousness that comes from obedience turns us toward God. Who wouldn't want to be obedient?

But, I've saved the best reason to obey for last. The best reason to obey is simply to show our love for God. 1 John 5:3 says, "This is love for God: to obey His commands. And His commands are not burdensome." So even while we may feel we can't listen, obey, then learn (LOL), WE CAN!  There's a promise right from Scripture—God's commands are not burdensome.  When you are called to do something, it is not intended to stress you.  It might help you grow, bring you blessings, or encourage someone else, but whatever it is, obedience shows love for God.  That's something I'd like to do daily.

Keep Laughing Out Loud, and keep Listening, Obeying, and Learning.

(August 2008)

# You Are What You Eat

Oh, the joy of choosing a new topic.  The month of the year has a large impact on the topic I choose, and it's so tempting, in February, to continue the conversation on New Year's resolutions.  Then there's the temptation to latch onto Valentine's Day, and write something about loving your partner.  Happily, the movie *Fire Proof* has done a fantastic job doing that.  If you haven't yet seen that movie, I strongly encourage you to do so.  But, I've opted to return to my Junior High days, in the 1970's, when signs hung outside the cafeteria that read, You Are What You Eat.

That was a new concept then.  A new adage to make you think about what you eat. Eat junk food, have a junky body.  Eat healthy, be healthy. I doubt it had any great effect on what I ate on a daily basis.  Back then I was a skinny Lynny and didn't really worry about the healthiness of what I ate, as long as I didn't gain weight—I was just reaching that age.

But, we're going to take a look at this from a Scriptural viewpoint.  We'll begin with the food side of it. Are there any hunters or fishermen out there?  Personally, I know hunters, and have eaten fresh venison thanks to these people, but I'm not a hunter or fisher.

Even so, I do know that some varmints are just not good eating. Raccoons, for instance, are scavengers. They eat garbage—literally, they'll push over garbage cans and eat whatever they can find that they can digest. Catfish, for the fishermen out there, unless raised on corn, are bottom feeders. Because of this, both these are considered really bad eating. Any country girl or boy can tell you, you just don't eat 'coon or catfish, because they don't taste good.

But I think, if you're hungry enough, anything tastes good. My example, as you can imagine, is hardly dramatic, because I've pretty much always been fed. But, when I was in labor with my second child, I ate my supper about 6:00 one night. I went into labor five hours later. I got to the hospital about 6:00 a.m., at which time, my son changed his mind. Labor basically stopped. So I walked and I got in the whirlpool and I tried anything to get labor going again. In the meantime, I missed breakfast. But, I was awake and active, and acutely aware that I had missed a meal.

Now, there are many of you out there who know that you are not allowed to eat when in the middle of labor, or any other kind of medical procedure. But I was hungry! I asked for food. No. I begged for food. No. I moped. No.

Finally, a sweet, angelic nurse smuggled me some red jell-o. Excuse me? While I greatly appreciated the kindness of this sweet woman, I don't especially like jell-o. At the same time, it had been about 18 hours with nothing but ice, so I ate it. And it was wonderful! I had never tasted anything so good in my life. When you're hungry, you'll eat whatever you can find.

Now it's time to look at this Scripturally. If you're eating gossip, it might taste good going down. It's fun to hear about things, and possibly even pass them on. But what does that do to your digestion?

If you're hanging onto unforgiveness, then you're going to be swallowing bitterness. It can't even taste good. But, we eat it. Over and over. We even bring it up again so we can rechew it. Yuck! But we do that. I've done that. I've heard it from others. I have a sweet woman in my life who is still bitter over some financial matters that took place almost 20 years ago. In that time, many people at whom she was angry have passed away. She's still bitter. Who is she hurting? The others have passed on, and still she sits, chewing on her bitterness and being miserable. Like I said, it doesn't even taste good, but we choose to feed on unforgiveness.

And remember, we are what we eat. So we're bitter and ugly. We look for opportunities to be mean. We take opportunities to be sarcastic. We enjoy teasing others and pointing out others' errors, even minor and insignificant ones. We're basically unlikable, even to ourselves, but we sit there and continue to feed at the same trough.

But, try eating Scripture. If you run to your Bible at least once a day; if you wake up and think, "Yes, I get to continue my Bible study today;" if you look forward to reviewing the Bible verses you copy into a notebook or onto note cards, then you're eating well! You're eating goodness, faithfulness, kindness. And, you will be healthy for it.

Your first thoughts when someone errs are that you know what they meant, so there's no reason to point it out. When someone starts a sentence with, "Maybe I shouldn't say this . . . ", you'll stop them and say, "then please don't," rather than be a party to gossip. You'll look for the good in others and find reasons to like people. You'll read, day after day, how Jesus acted and behaved, how much God loves you, and how you can win souls to Christ. And you'll act on it. You'll be loveable because you'll love others as Christ did.

Further, try serving the Lord. Again, you'll be filled with goodness, and it will be reflected in you. You are what you eat, and you're a servant. Servants are humble. They have to be. When you are giving of yourself, you are sweet. Now, sweetness is something you want to eat. Whether you're serving at church, your kids' school, a local hospital, it doesn't matter. Whether volunteering is a regular thing on your calendar or you fit in volunteering when you can, it doesn't matter. The point is to serve the Lord, from where you are. Maybe you can't be on the next church mission trip to Africa, but maybe you can pray for those saints who are going. That's serving! From where you are.

This service might encourage you to review your gift of the Spirit. I guarantee you, when you accepted Jesus as your personal Savior, you were given at least one gift. Take an inventory if you're unsure of the gift you received. That way you can serve in a way where you're gifted. What a double blessing—one to you, one to the receiver of your service.

Another way of saying you are what you eat is that you reap what you sow. Sow goodness, grow goodness. Sow Bible memorization, reap comfort. May February be a new wonderful start to your year.
(February 2009)

# Jesus was Born to . . .

December is a great month, from beginning to end, and I don't mean because we open Christmas gifts on the 25<sup>th</sup>. This was, in our way of thinking, the last month of Mary's gestation of Jesus (ignoring the difference of calendars over the past 2000 years). That means, our Savior is soon to be born—well, the anniversary of His birth. My husband reminds me annually that we don't have birthdays, we have anniversaries.

In my personal Bible study, I'm studying Daniel. This book of the Old Testament leads to talk about end times, because Daniel and Revelation are sister books.

In my study, I can't help but share what I learn with my family. I get so tickled when I read this amazing book that I have to share what I learn with whomever is close enough to listen. Independently, all three of my cherubs have asked me, "If God knew what was going to happen, why did He make Lucifer in the first place? Why did He allow sin to enter the world?" I loved answering them, each with their own example.

The point is, God doesn't want robots whom He commands to worship and praise Him. With my daughter, I used her Barbie dolls. Remember when we were little, and played dolls? As I got older, I spent more time arranging the furniture in the house and less time actually playing with the dolls.  But through it all, for all the years I played with them, I imagined what it would be like to have my dolls come to life and live in the home I had created for them.  And I was creative with what I had.  I used my brothers' blocks for the walls, and an empty tissue box became both a bed when upside down, and a car when it was turned over.  If I could have spoken things into existence, like our Heavenly Father, my dolls would have lived in a palace!

But, I asked my 15 year old, as much fun as it would have been to have those dolls come to life, would you want them to love you because you commanded them to love you, or to love you because they choose to love you, from their heart?  With my youngest I asked him if he wanted his stuffties, especially his beloved Durkos, to love him because they have to, or because they want to. All three of my cherubs, each with their own example, clearly understand that they want to be loved because of who they are, not because robots are commanded to love.

Well, it's the same thing for us.  The Lord allowed sin to enter the world, but He already had the plan.  How often do we not come up with a way out until we're trapped?  Not God.  In Harper's Bible Dictionary, this is explained:  "God has a plan and purpose for His world. Providence is not a principle of orderliness or reason; rather, providence is the will of the Creator who is actively involved in moving His creation to a goal. History is not a cyclical process of endless repetition; history is being moved toward the predetermined end."

He knew what was going to happen, and has already determined the conclusion.  In fact, the Trinity knew what was going to happen.  Yes, Jesus was there in the beginning (Genesis 1:1 and John 1:1, so both the Old and New Testaments are covered and are consistent).

The plan was made before sin came anywhere near Adam and Eve.

And that's what Christmas is all about, it's part of God's original plan.  Jesus was only born for one reason—to die.  And we celebrate His birth, because without His birth, we would have no way to get into Heaven.  John 14:6 says, "I am the way, the truth, and the life; no one comes to the Father but through Me."  If Jesus hadn't been born as a baby, and grown into a man, He wouldn't have died on that ugly cross and descended into hell for three days, paying the price for our sins.  He is our bridge to heaven.

You know, as a teacher for years and years, I've taught thousands of students.  The majority of those students came into class, prepared to do the work and earn their grade.  But sometimes, I would get one who wanted to get the grade by going around me.  Students sometimes see the teacher as the barrier to their grade.  Like we have a pile of A's behind us, and we're doing our best to block the students from getting there.

In fact, we do have an endless supply of grades of all kinds, A's through F's.  But my goal is to pave a clear road the students simply have to walk to and collect their A at the end of the semester.  I lay it all out in my syllabus on day one:  attend class, participate, write well written papers and turn them in on time, work in a group on a project, and collect your grade.  The majority of students get it.  But the ones who wanted to turn in a single page of notes written at the last minute, and then demand an A, because the C was only given to them because I had something against them, always amazed me.   They thought they knew a better way to the grade—do it their way, and demand the grade they wanted.

It's the same thing with heaven.  The Bible has clearly laid out the road to salvation, but it's a lot more narrow than my syllabus.  **A**ccept Jesus as your Savior, **B**elieve He died on the cross for you personally, and

Commit your life to Him. A, B, C, 1, 2, 3, it's done. But people want to create their own agenda. They add attending church, being baptized, doing good works, giving away money—and many more things. Now, these are all good things to do, but none of them will get you to Heaven, according to the Bible. We can't change John 14:6 to say, I am the way, the truth, and the life; no one comes to the Father but through Me, *unless you do enough good works and give to the poor and attend a certain church, then I'll let you in.* It doesn't work that way! ABC, keep it simple.

We're going to celebrate Christmas in a few short weeks. I declare days go faster in December and during vacations. This celebration is about Jesus' birth. Jesus was born for the sole purpose of dying for you. Praise the Lord for His great plan of salvation.
(December 2008)

# If . . . Then Promises

I have been collecting Scripture for this article for months and months.  In gathering for so long, I have reaped a bountiful harvest!  In fact, I have too much information.  So, after many hours of prayer, let's wade through only a small fraction of the If . . . Then promises in the Bible.

First, what am I talking about?  Well, there are a plethora of promises in the Bible.  You probably know many of them.  For instance, Deuteronomy 31:6b says, " . . . for the Lord your God goes with you.  He will never leave you nor forsake you."  Now, you may know the address as Hebrews 13:5, because the unknown author of Hebrews quoted it.  I think it's important to use the Old Testament citation because the quote refers to our Heavenly Father, not Jesus.  Of course, Jesus will never leave you nor forsake you, either, but it wasn't originally a Messianic promise.

Other Biblical promises include: Psalm 23:3  - "He restores my soul." Matthew 28:30 - "Surely I am with you always, to the very end of the age."  2 Corinthians 12:9a - "My grace is sufficient for you." Psalm 32:7 – "You are my hiding place; You will protect me from trouble and surround me with songs of deliverance."

Psalm 119:130 – "The unfolding of your words gives light; it gives understanding to the simple."

These last two are promises that first David (author of Psalm 32) and then a Poet (author of Psalm 119) claim. They are holding the Lord accountable. That's brave. It's also trusting, and something we can do, too.

These are all great promises that we can claim as Christians, only because we've accepted Jesus as our Personal Savior. We don't have to do anything. It's just the Lord's love and mercy, pouring over us.

But, there are lots of lots of promises in the Bible that come with a clause. Because of the differences in language (Aramaic, Hebrew, and Greek versus English), some of them are written backwards, but they're still there. There are far too many to discuss in one article or seminar, but let's look at some of them. You can make it a goal to highlight the If . . . Then promises in your Bible as you come across them in your daily reading.

Even John 3:16, made famous by sports fans, is a promise predicated on an If statement. It reads, "For God so loved the world that He gave His only begotten Son, that whoever believes in Him should not perish but have everlasting life." Did you find the clause? We have to believe in the Son in order to not perish. God has no grandchildren.

Let's go to the Old Testament, so please turn to Exodus 20. Some of you will immediately realize we're smack in the middle of the 10 Commandments. Let's scroll down to the fifth commandment, in verse 12: "Honor your father and your mother, so that you may live long in the land the Lord your God is giving you."

Let's stop and think about this. If you honor your father and mother, you may live long in the land your God gave you. Now, we don't think about living long in the land today, but the meaning is still there. If we honor our parents, we may live long.  Okay, this is just a start.  Let's keep going.

Joshua 1:8-9 says, "Do not let this Book of the Law depart from your mouth; meditate on it day and night, so that you may be careful to do everything written in it.  Then you will be prosperous and successful."

Wow, we've hit a huge promise here.  We will be prosperous and successful!  Isn't that what we all want for ourselves, and our children, and even our siblings and friends?  But, you can't take Scripture away from its context, which is why the first part is so important.  The Lord is telling Joshua that IF he doesn't forget what he knows from the book of the Law, IF he meditates on it day and night, and IF he's careful to do everything written in it, THEN he will be prosperous and successful.

Now, we need to remember that, thanks to Jesus' sacrifice on the cross, we don't have to obey the 629 laws that existed in the Old Testament.  But, we are told, again in the first Psalm, verse two, to meditate on the Lord's law day and night.  IF we do, then we will be like a tree planted by streams of water, and whatever we do will prosper.  (I've written before on the redundancy of Scripture, and here it is again.) So while we may not have to exactly memorize the original laws, we do want to meditate and obey Scripture. By the way, I've found it much easier to meditate and obey Scripture when I memorize it, but that's another article.

Let's look at more If . . . Then promises: 2 Chronicles 13:18 – "The men of Israel were subdued on that occasion, and the men of Judah were victorious **because** they relied on the Lord, the God of their fathers."  1 Chronicles 5:20 – "They were helped in fighting them, and God handed the Hagrites and all their allies over to them, **because** they cried out to Him during the battle.  He answered their prayers, **because** they trusted in Him."

So you see, sometimes the promises are backwards, but they are there. The last one above could be written, IF they cried to Him during battle, God helped them fight. IF they trusted in Him, He answered their prayers.

Does God love you any less, and want any less for you, than He did for these people who lived thousands of years ago? Of course not. These promises are as valid today as they were when God made them generations and generations ago. Remember, a thousand years to us is a day to Him (2 Peter 3:8). And the battles we fight today are as real as the wars these people were fighting. So our fight may be with finances, jobs, or society, but they are still battles, and **If** we rely on the Lord, and **If** we cry out to Him, we will be victorious.

One section of Scripture that has gotten me through some bad days is Jeremiah 29:11-13. It starts with a promise in verse 11: "For I know the plans I have for you," declares the Lord. "plans to prosper you and not to harm you, plans to give you hope and a future." Verse 12: "Then you will call upon Me and come and pray to Me, and I will listen to you." IF we call upon God and pray to God, He will listen to us. We have to pray and call first. In Verse 13: "You will seek Me and find Me when you seek Me with all your heart." Again, when we seek with all our heart, we will find God.

There's the if-then. Reading it backwards, IF you seek Me (God) with all your heart, THEN you will find Me (God). It's not enough to just look around; you need to SEEK. Let's stop and look at this section for another minute. The definition of the word seek is "to try to achieve or obtain something. To go toward a place or thing (Webster)."

You don't ever accidentally seek something. It's a deliberate action, because you're trying to achieve something; you're making an effort to move toward something. When we make an effort to move toward

God, we will find Him.  He's waiting for us, with arms outstretched and aching to hold us.

One negative thought, but I'd be remiss to ignore it:  If things aren't going so well, you may want to consider if you're doing your part, and not just waiting for the Lord to do what you want Him to do.  We do have responsibility in our lives.

There are so many more If . . . Then promises in the Bible, and you may have noticed, we barely touched the New Testament yet.  I promise you (pun intended) that there's a goldmine of promises waiting for you. Enjoy finding each one, dear saints, and enjoy receiving the Promises of God.

(October 2008)

# Being Thankful for What We Have, Not What We Want

I was surprised and tickled to read recently from Beth Moore that she's sad she can't sing. I have so much respect for this lady's teaching, and she's upset over not being able to sing. Now we have something else in common. I've always been sad that I can't sing, but then, I'm no Beth Moore.

The next day I had to leave a coffee clutch in my driveway to pick up our youngest son from choir. A well-intentioned neighbor asked if I sing and if musical talent runs in the family. I assured her I can't sing, saying, "While some of my siblings have musical ability, I got the beauty." She laughed as she was supposed to.

Then, the next day my son heard me singing in the shower, and asked about the song. It was something I'd sung once in high school, more than 20 years ago. Okay, more than 25 years ago. My oldest son commented about how I could remember words from a song I've heard once so long ago, and I replied, "God has given me an amazing ability to remember the words to songs." By the way, since I can't sing a note, this is proof that God has a sense of humor.

I mentioned that it's funny how we always want what we don't have, like Beth and me wanting the gift of song. But, what about the gifts we have? Beth has an amazing gift in her teaching. I have a sense of humor. In fact, the day in Bible study that I read about Beth's wish for music, the woman next to me touched my arm and remarked that I'm such a funny person. I had just made some comment that was found witty by the group.

The question is, as much as I wish I had the ability to sing, would I give up my sense of humor and wit? I LOVE that I can make people laugh. It's one of the things I like best about myself. Trust me, it's a short list, but at least that's one thing I can always find on it. I guess I wouldn't trade, because humor is how God gave me, and able to sing He did not!
(November 2007)

# Born to . . .

By the time you're reading this, it's been about a month since the horrific incident at Virginia Tech, but for me, it's been only a week. This seems personal to me, because I graduated from Tech many years ago. As the media discussed Ambler-Johnston Hall, I could remember where it is located, and remember friends from that dorm. I passed it on the way to my boyfriend's dorm. I've walked the halls. As they discussed the drill field, I can't remember how many times I crossed it—a thousand? Even back then, I could envision the early years of the college, and imagine the cadets drilling. Virginia Tech has a long-standing history, and now it's been marred.

The truth is, there were a lot of victims that day. Not just the ones we buried, but the families who have been left to live without their babies. Yes, even college-aged children are babies to their mommies. This is a wake up call to use our time here wisely. Why are we on this earth?

I've found the worldly view to be very negative—akin to, whoever dies with the most toys, wins. It can be overly materialistic and dog-eat-dog. The Christian realm doesn't have to be negative, but we still have to live within the constructs of this world. Our challenge is to live our lives in a Godly fashion.

It has been suggested that if somebody had put a stop to the bullying, or come alongside the shooter when he was younger, the massacre may not have happened. Of course, we'll never know. But, what if somebody had stood up to the bullies on behalf of a student, or asked the less popular people to join them at a party? Would it really hurt to have one more person in the group? Even if such actions don't completely prevent the tragedies that are taking place in this world, they would make this a better world in which to live.

Insecurity doesn't end in school. In neighborhoods, offices, stores, and everywhere across the country, somebody is on the outside looking in. We may not even realize it. Look around and see who might enjoy an invitation to lunch, or would like to go window-shopping, just for the camaraderie. You'll benefit from having a new friend as much as they'll benefit from having you as a friend.

The great commission in Matthew 28 tells us to make disciples of all nations. We're here for a short time, and without any warning, that time can end abruptly. Let's use the tragedies not to lament, but to encourage us to use our time wisely, for His kingdom. (May 2007)

# The Roman Road

In my life, I tend to use Christian words, and if someone picks up on them, I know we have something special in common. I even do this with complete strangers. Recently I received a call, despite being on the no-call list, and was solicited for money. I explained that our giving (I call it tithe, from the Old Testament concept of giving 10%, which is the definition of tithe, one tenth) goes to spreading the gospel, so that people may have the joy of knowing Jesus in this life, and the confidence of eternity in heaven.

Saints, Praise the Lord, I was shocked by the response I received that day. Usually I get a very gentle response, saying the person is already saved, or assuring me I'm doing important work. In this case, the woman was . . . intrigued. So I ventured a bit further, explaining that salvation is for everyone, the children for whom she was raising funds, adults, and her.

She then asked if there were organizations that do that. I assured her there are thousands of them! I asked if she has access to a Bible, and was told she has three of them at home. So I quoted John 14:6 to her: Jesus answered, "I am the way, the truth, and the life. No one comes to the Father except through Me." She was happy to hear this!  I declare that she wrote down the reference, and told me she was going to look it up in one of those Bibles when she got home that night.  Wow!  Based on her voice, I'm guessing she was raised in the United States, and she had never heard even a word of the Gospel.

I've wanted to write an article on salvation for some time.  While I tend to toss the word around, I can't be sure everyone shares the same meaning.

There are many ways to discuss the Gospel.  When my children went to VBS, Vacation Bible School for other moms like me who had no personal experience with it and, in fact, had never heard of it until I had children, they learned the ABC approach.  **A**ccept Jesus; **B**elieve He died on the cross for you; **C**onfess your sins.  Campus Crusade for Christ, a program that exists in many Colleges and High Schools across the country, uses the four questions, or tenets, approach.  Calvinists may have learned the five points.  They all work, especially when explained lovingly, calmly, and rationally without censure or judgment.

The goal of anyone sharing the gospel of Christ is to ensure that people know, understand, and believe the truth of the Bible.  Years after I was saved, I heard of the Roman Road, and thought we would take this trip together.  Whether you've newly come to Christ, or made your decision to follow Him years ago, it's always a lovely journey.

There are four stops on this road, and they're not in order in the book of Romans, which is a New Testament book, the second one after the four gospels.  So the books of the New Testament start as follows:  Matthew, Mark, Luke, and John, Acts and Romans—and we're there!  By the way, when I taught my children to memorize the books of the New Testament, something I learned so that I could teach them, I used a very loose version of the song ten little Indians.  It helps.

Our first stop is Romans 3:23 – "For all have sinned and fall short of the glory of God." Sure enough, when sharing the gospel of Christ, I have come upon people who claimed that they couldn't be saved because God didn't know how bad they'd been in their life. Excuse me? I may not know their past, and you may not know their past, but if anyone knows, it's God! That's why we begin here, to prove, through Scripture, that ALL have sinned. There is nothing, NOTHING, that anyone has done or can do that the Lord doesn't already know, and, AND, has already forgiven!

From failing to return the item you picked up off the floor when you were a child, to mean thoughts in adolescence, to bad decisions in adulthood, the Father knows it all. And, He loves us anyway. I promise, I have the same history, and He forgave me every one of the sins I have committed, and will commit. Yes, I'm still sinning. Not as intentionally, maybe, but I know from overreacting to being irritated at other drivers, sins are still coming, and will continue, until I go home someday. The difference is that I'm forgiven now and need not feel condemnation (Romans 8:1, which isn't one of the stops on our journey, but it's a great verse!).

So we're all in good (bad) company, in that every one of us is a sinner. There's nothing that God doesn't know and He loves you, exactly as you are. How awesome is that? Recognizing this truth, we're ready to move to stop two: Romans 6:23 – "For the wages of sin is death, but the gift of God is eternal life in Christ Jesus our Lord."

Yep, there it is in black and white, in the greatest book ever written. We deserve to die. And by that, it means to burn in h, e, double hockey sticks. That's what we deserve for being sinners. If you're perfect, you get to go to heaven—I didn't make that up, it's written in the Old Testament. There were over 600 laws that had to be followed, and nobody, nobody (I know, I'm using a lot of repetition to make points today) could do it.

But that's okay, because God has a better idea. Rather than us trying to live up to, and earn the ability to go to heaven, God makes it a free gift. We're getting ahead of ourselves, because that's stop number three on the Roman Road: Romans 5:8 – "But God demonstrates His own love for us in this: While we were still sinners, Christ died for us."

Again, that's amazing! God has the perfect way to get us to heaven—He sent His Son to bear our sins. Christ died for you, dear saint. Put your name in that last sentence, instead of the word saint. Christ died for you, _____. Yes, He did! Wow! That's serious love. In my life, as a mommy, I would rather suffer myself than see my children in pain, yet that's what our sweet Lord did for us. Can you relate?

That leads us to our last stop on the Roman Road: Romans 10:9-11 – "That if you confess with your mouth, "Jesus is Lord," and believe in your heart that God raised Him from the dead, you will be saved. For it is with your heart that you believe and are justified, and it is with your mouth that you confess and are saved."

The first time I read Romans 10:9, I just stared at it in amazement. Here was the entire gospel, in one verse. And then I wondered, why don't people hold up signs with this verse on it at football games? I really did. John 3:16, "For God so loved the world He gave His only begotten Son, that whoever believes in Him will not perish but have everlasting life," is a great verse! That's the sign you see at sports events. It's a great verse, and it tells you that God loves you, but it doesn't tell you how to get to heaven. It's all here in Romans 10, though. Let's consider it together.

"Confess with your mouth, Jesus is Lord." Did you say it out loud?

Whether you want to say it aloud or silently, right now, say the words, "Jesus is Lord." That's right. He's not a prophet, or just another man. He's the Lord. He was there in the beginning, in Genesis 1:1—"In the beginning, God created the heavens and the earth." The word used for God in this verse, the first of the Bible, is plural, because in the beginning, the Father, Son, and Holy Spirit were all present. The New Testament confirms this in John 1:1 – "In the beginning was the Word, and the Word was with God and the Word was God." If you have questions about to whom the Word applies, verse 14 makes it clear it's Jesus.

I can't tell you how many people have told me, "It's not that easy." Well, yes and no. It is that easy to have your name written in the Book of Life. You accept and believe, in your heart and mind, that Jesus died on the cross for you. My husband points out that some people miss heaven by 13 inches, the distance from your mind to your heart. They know in their brains that Jesus came, died on the cross, and rose again, but never quite accept it in their heart. That's why Romans 10 is so important. It clearly states the need to believe in your heart as well.

Once your name is written in the book of life, and you have the assurance of salvation, there's no assurance of an easy walk on earth. In fact, the evil one may do his best to derail you. But you're stronger than that, because you can call on the strength of the Holy Spirit any time you want, once you've accepted Jesus as your personal savior. Knowing you're going to heaven makes it easier to tolerate some of the experiences of this world, because this world will no longer be your home. You have a beautiful mansion waiting for you in heaven, in which to dwell for all eternity. I pray, dear saints, that I see each of you there, and we spend eternity together, worshiping our heavenly Father.
(July 2009)

# Full Obedience

In 1 Sam 15:1-10 Samuel said to Saul, "I am the one the Lord sent to anoint you king over His people Israel; so listen (with a view to obeying) now to the message from the Lord.  This is what the Lord Almighty says:  "I will punish the Amalekites for what they did to Israel when they waylaid them as they came up from Egypt.  Now go, attack the Amalekites and *totally destroy (emphasis mine)* everything that belongs to them.  Do not spare them; put to death men and women, children and infants, cattle and sheep, camels and donkeys.'"

So Saul summoned the men and mustered them at Telaim—two hundred thousand foot soldiers and ten thousand men from Judah.  Saul went to the city of Amalek and set an ambush in the ravine.  Then he said to the Kenites, "Go away, leave the Amalekites so that I do not destroy you along with them; for you showed kindness to all the Israelites when they came up out of Egypt,"  so the Kenites moved away from the Amalekites.

Then Saul attacked the Amalekites all the way from Havilah to Shur, to the east of Egypt.  He took Agag king of the Amalekites alive, and all his people he totally destroyed with the sword.  But Saul and the army spared

Agag and the best of the sheep and cattle, the fat calves and lambs—everything that was good. These they were unwilling to destroy completely, but everything that was despised and weak they totally destroyed.

Then the word of the Lord came to Samuel: I am grieved that I have made Saul king, because he has turned away from Me and has not carried out My instructions."

Anything less than full obedience is disobedience and GRIEVES the LORD.

That's my thesis in this article. Anything less than full obedience is disobedience. It's like the adage, Half a Truth is a Whole Lie. Do you remember that one? A few friends and I shared that thought in High School, but we were the weird ones. No, we weren't Christians and it wasn't on Christian principles we believed it. We just found that adage and believed it. But, other girls found us strict and exacting. White lies don't hurt, right? It's for a good reason, right? It wasn't until years later that I came to Christ, and years after that when I found this verse and concept in the Bible.

Let's see how we feel when people we know, neighbors, colleagues, or children, treat us this way. We ask somebody to do something for us, and they kind of sort of do it, but not quite. It's when we ask our children to do the dishes, knowing we mean to clean the kitchen, and we return to find dishes in the dishwasher, but the counter unwiped, the floor unswept, and the room just not clean. That's less than full obedience, but they have you on a technicality. Do you find that funny? Amusing? Insightful on their part? Were you proud of their legalistic abilities?

God doesn't like it either. In fact, in 1 Sam 15:22, it says, "But Samuel replied (to Saul): "Does the Lord delight in burnt offerings and sacrifices as much as in obeying the voice of the Lord? To obey is better than sacrifice, and to heed is better than the fat of rams.""

We can't explain away our disobedience, or choose to obey in another way (but I offered the cattle in sacrifice just doesn't cut it).

So while the Lord wants full obedience, even when we err, there's still something to be done. The best thing to do when we're found in disobedience, is to admit it.

"Yes, I did that." Four little words, but they can be so hard to say!

Second, apologize.

"Yes, I did that, and I'm sorry." Three words added behind the first four, but what an impact they'll have! Admit and apologize—what a strong combination.

Third, rectify.

"Yes, I did that. I'm sorry. What can I do?"

That shows true remorse. You're willing to try to undo any damage. You've taken the burden back upon yourself. That shows maturity.

The Lord wants full obedience, but He doesn't always get it. He didn't get it from the Israelites, he didn't get it from great men of the Bible (do some research on Moses, Saul, and David), and He doesn't always get it from us. But PTL, He does offer us second chances. The goal is to make up for our disobedience when we can, and put forth the effort to live in 100% obedience in the future.

Remember, according to 1 Sam 15:35, "Until the day Samuel died, he did not go to see Saul again, though Samuel mourned for him. And the Lord was grieved that He had made Saul king over Israel." This is years later and the Lord was still grieved. Let's do our best to live in obedience, so that we won't grieve our Lord.

# When We're Mistaught

Once upon a time, long, long ago, when we were young, our brains were a blank slate. On these slates people, mostly our parents and family at first, and then teachers and pastors and friends, eventually colleagues and news media and all other sources, would write. This is how we learned, matured, and developed.

Because the people who were doing the original writing loved us and wanted us to grow to be independent and successful adults, they taught us to the best of their abilities. No parents ever intentionally mistaught their child the order of the alphabet, right? But, over time, things change. For instance, using not our alphabet but a foreign alphabet, it turns out I could not correctly teach my children the alphabet I learned in 8th grade when they took their foreign language requirement 30 years later. Sure enough, this other alphabet had changed and some of the letters no longer exist. So while I had no intention of misteaching my children, without better, up-to-date information, I would have mistaught my children.

Now, that's a very obvious example. Not all situations are so obvious. But I'm becoming aware that more and more of what I was taught, and what I have taught, is no longer completely accurate. Even worse, in some cases it is still correct, but in others, it isn't. Or, it correctly applies to some people, but not others.

I hope I haven't lost you. Let's get specific. I have half a dozen examples of misteachings of which I'm acutely aware today and I'd like to briefly discuss a few of these, followed by what to do when you find yourself in similar straits. Let's begin.

Because of the current state of our economy, and the number of people who have approached me recently about careers, let's start with how to find a job. In my olden days, way back in the 80's, I knew how to find a job. It was all about getting that Sunday paper and spending Sunday afternoon typing cover letters and copying resumes. Not all jobs were found through the Sunday paper, but enough were that it was a legitimate mode of communication.

Have you seen a job section in a Sunday paper lately? It's thin. The rules for how to find a job have changed. Now you need to be on-line and signed up with any and/or all of the career opportunities networks out there. And networking is an even better way to find a job! The adage, "it's not what you know, it's who you know," has actually never been more true. And if you don't know them personally, find someone who does and connect with them. The computer again makes this easy—but it's not what anybody my age was originally taught! The rules changed when we weren't looking.

This has been hard on some students of mine. I have a great example of a student who just graduated from College. He had been taking the advice of his Dad, until he realized, it wasn't working! He called me, and much to his father's chagrin, met with me to discuss his job search. I gently explained that his father hadn't intentionally mislead him, but that the rules had changed in the 30 years since his dad had looked for a job, so the information he shared was just out of date. Not an intentional foul, but misteaching nonetheless.

Okay, example number two: communication. Of course we all learned to communicate, but we didn't all learn to do it well. The way people learn to communicate is by watching how it is modeled. If your family is full of yellers, you'll learn that yelling is an acceptable, even appropriate, means of communication. If whining gets you your way, then even as an adult, you may use this as a primary means of communication. But what happens in the business world, or in adult relationships, when our means of communication isn't acceptable, or doesn't work? We need to relearn how to communicate. How? First, by watching methods that do work. I remember hearing one colleague say to another, "I hear what you're saying, but I'm making a decision to go in another direction." Wow, that stopped me in my tracks! The person acknowledged the other's ideas, but made it clear that the decision was his responsibility and he would go another route. I could do that, now that I had heard it. I would never have been able to come up with it on my own.

But what if we don't even know we've been mistaught? Jumping into the Christian message here, what if we were mistaught how to get into heaven? Please don't be upset if you're learning here for the first time that you can't earn your way into heaven. Ephesians 2:8-9 makes it very clear: "For it is by grace you have been saved, through faith—and this not from yourselves, it is the gift of God—not by works, so that no one can boast." If we could earn our way to heaven, we could then boast in our good works, and this verse clearly negates that thought. Romans 9:16 echoes the thought: "It does not, therefore, depend on man's desire or effort, but on God's mercy."

The entire gospel is given in Romans 10:9: "That if you confess with your mouth, "Jesus is Lord," and believe in your heart that God raised Him from the dead, you will be saved." Once you truly meditate on this verse, you'll see that if you were mistaught, the truth is

154

here—you have to admit you're a sinner (Romans 3:23), believe that Jesus died on the cross for you, confess Him as Lord, and ask Jesus to live in your heart. No matter what you were taught, this is the truth of it.

The famous verse of John 3:16 states clearly that God loved the world so much that He gave His only begotten Son that whoever believes in Jesus doesn't have to go to h, e, double hockey sticks. And John 14:6 has Jesus, Himself, saying the ONLY WAY to get to heaven is to accept Him as your personal Savior.

Or maybe you weren't mistaught that works will get you into heaven, but you just never heard the message that you have to have a personal relationship with Jesus. For all the stories and messages you heard, John 14:6 never seemed to be mentioned. That's not exactly mistaught, it's more non-taught. God is aware of your need to hear the truth, and you'll hear it, as promised is Romans 1:20, "For since the creation of the world God's invisible qualities—His eternal power and divine nature—have been clearly seen, being understood from what has been made, so that men are without excuse."

As a teenager, years before I would come to saving knowledge of Christ, I was asked point blank if I was going to heaven. At the time I didn't know I wasn't, and I tried to dodge the question, but was told it was a yes or no answer. So I answered in the affirmative. Then I was told that I could never go to heaven because I had told God what to do. Excuse me? Talk about being set up.

On a wee bit easier level, what if we were mistaught how to pray? I've had people say to me, "I don't know how to pray." The obvious answer is that prayer is just talking with God, yet I heard a sermon once where the Pastor very specifically said that prayer is not talking with God—how do we reconcile fact and fiction?

Well, the first thing to do is GO TO THE WORD. Yep, that's where you're going to find the answers for yourself. Don't rely on others to interpret Scripture for you. Read it yourself. There are lots of commentaries out there to help you, but reading it for yourself will give you an intimacy you can't get anywhere else.

In the case of being told I can't go to heaven because I told God what to do, the teenager who told me that might not have read the truth himself. In fact, the Bible clearly outlines how to get to heaven, and it clearly states that God can't lie, or else He wouldn't be perfect. So in fact, we can accept Jesus as our Savior, know that we're destined for heaven, and tell others about it. How do I know? I've read it.

Still, there are other ways to learn if you've been mistaught. Proverbs 15:22 tells us that wisdom is found in counsel: "Plans fail for lack of counsel, but with many advisers they succeed." In 1 Kings 22:5, Jehoshophat also said to the king of Israel, "First seek the counsel of the Lord." So find a counselor. Look for someone to mentor you. Call a friend and ask to be accountability partners. You'll learn and grow by surrounding yourself with others who are more mature.

General study is a great way to learn general truths. Even if you're not trying to learn the answer to a specific question, learn and study the Bible just to see what you don't know. "The fear (respect) of the Lord is the beginning of wisdom," Psalms 111:10.

Prayer can answer a myriad of questions. When you don't know what to do, bring your questions before the Lord. He'll answer you one way or another, and you'll learn and grow in the truth. For a great model of prayer, go to Matthew 6:9, where you'll find what is commonly called the Our Father. Prayer can also be greatly accomplished with the acronym ACTS – Adoration of the Lord, Confession of your sins, Thanksgiving for your blessings, and Supplication, where you state your requests. Remember, Jesus cried out to His Daddy,

Abba, the night before He faced the cross, recognizing that all things are possible through the Father. Jesus then continued to say, "but not My will, but Thy will be done," Mark 14:36. Pray, but pray in God's will.

Be open to new ideas and concepts. I have made myself open to lots of ideas in my life, but as I study and learn, I reject the ideas that are contrary to Scripture. You can't serve two masters, and I choose to follow the living God. Therefore, I can't embrace any edicts that counterfeit or oppose the truth of Scripture. But, there are lots of ideas that can co-exist—don't allow yourself to get caught up in those discussions. Keep centered on what's important.

Memorize Scripture. Okay, this was a tough concept for me 25 years ago. I had never memorized Scripture growing up, and since I had a Bible, couldn't I just look up whatever I needed to know? Well, that worked for me until I came upon Philippians 4:6 –"be anxious about nothing, but in all things, through prayer and supplication, with thanksgiving, present your requests to the Lord." I found that verse and read it so many times—I had a HUGE issue with worry at the time—that I memorized it. And I learned that I LIKED knowing the verse. I could recall it any time, whether or not I had a Bible in my hand. And when other people were telling me their problems, I could recite it to them, and they felt better. After that, I was on my way. I've had peaks and valleys with Bible memorization, but it's something I still do today, and I still love.

The next idea is rather hard to hear, so please be ready—avoid unhealthy people. So many of us learn things from our family, and while we've grown and matured and are ready to accept truth over what we thought was real, not everyone has matured with us. So, it may be better that you avoid sharing your thoughts with people who don't have your best interests in mind, or who aren't very supportive of you, even if they share your blood type. Proverbs 18:24b – " . . . but there is a friend who sticks closer than a brother." The Lord included this verse in Scripture for a reason, and I can't be the only person in the history of the world who's needed to hear it. I'm not saying you can't celebrate holidays with these people, but avoid certain conversations when you do see them if they're going to tear you down.

Finally, decide now whom you'll serve ("But as for me and my household, we will serve the Lord," Joshua 24:15) and stand up for right. Even if you were mistaught something originally, it's never too late to learn the truth and stand on it. Educate yourself and you'll learn to not depart from it.

(September 2009)

# Accepting Gifts

It's hard to accept gifts.  Not on our birthdays or Christmas, when we actually expect them, but unexpected gifts.  For instance, a friend recently gave us $25 for helping her tote a new mattress home in our truck.  Our first inclination was to return the money, even though we did do the work, at no inconvenience to our friend, as we picked it up, delivered it, and even offered to set it up in the room where we delivered it; and as we had just learned we would lose a job soon, the amount of money, though small for this woman, would be nice for us.  We decided to keep the money and it became allowance money for a week.  That was huge to us, but we were ready to say no, mainly because we don't accept gifts well.

Why not?  I know from experience in gift-giving, and in conversation, that my husband and I, and even our children, are not the only ones who have trouble accepting gifts.  Sometimes it's not just gifts we have trouble accepting.

Our youngest, 12 at the time, was helping his Dad and Aunt run the Grandma's garage sale.  Our son's job was to help people carry their purchases down a very long driveway.  One woman kindly offered him a dollar for his service. My son's response was to say no thank you. The woman insisted and my son received a dollar tip. When he told me the story, he seemed both excited and embarrassed. I assured him he did the right thing, because the laborer is worthy of his wage. How was this different from my husband accepting $25 for his labor? It wasn't. It isn't.

So, why don't we accept gifts better? One reason, it causes some embarrassment, but I'm not sure why. Maybe it's the lack of reciprocity. If somebody hands us something, when it's not an expected time, like a wedding, we feel like we need to return the favor. So the fact that we were caught unaware might embarrass us. That's silly. The point of an I-love-you gift is to tell the other person that you love them, not look for an I-love-you gift in return. And when we're the ones giving the gift, are we expecting something in return? Of course not.

The idea of reciprocity leads to another reason people may not accept gifts well—it may lead to a feeling of having to repay. That doesn't make sense. A gift should come without strings attached. Otherwise it's not a gift, it's a trade. Growing up, if a friend invited me to spend the night, it was then my turn to invite her to spend the night, so we'd be even. I still see this with couples and families today, but usually with dinner parties, not sleepovers. But, if you look at the idea of a gift, the concept of reciprocity isn't there.

You can add your own ideas why some people don't accept gifts well. In fact, I'd like to hear them if you're willing to share. But, please know that gifts go all the way back to the Bible. I'm not talking about the Old Testament concept of gifts where vassal nations were required to gift other countries as a tribute. That was nothing more than payment for 1) not invading them, and 2) offering protection from the threat of other invading nations.

Jesus was brought gifts for years after His birth: Matthew 2:11 – "And they came into the house and saw the young child with Mary his mother; and they fell down and worshipped Him; and opening their treasures they offered unto Him gifts, gold and frankincense and myrrh."

Wow!  These were nice gifts from well respected people.  We're not going to discuss the significance of the gifts, but it's interesting if you want to look it up.  The point is, these rulers chose to gift Jesus with elaborate gifts.  Please remember, Joseph was a carpenter, so gifts of gold, frankincense, and myrrh probably weren't everyday items.

I have two questions.  One, why should we choose to give others gifts?  And, what is the proper response to gifts?

First, one reason to give a gift is appreciation.  If somebody does something kind for you, like toting an item, whether it's a mattress or a garage sale find, there's nothing wrong with showing appreciation through a gift.  It's not required, and I'm not suggesting you start giving gifts for every act of kindness.  I believe a heartfelt thank you is perfectly appropriate, too.  If we were to receive a gift for EVERY kindness, I think it could impede our motive in being kind.  We would start looking for and expecting the gift, and then it wouldn't be a gift, but an expectation.

Another reason to give somebody a gift is because they need it.  It may be an emotional or physical need.  When I was a Senior in College, I went home for a weekend.  By this time all my siblings were out of the house.  On Sunday, my parents took me out for brunch, then a surprise shopping trip, where they bought me a new blazer. Wow!  I remember my dad saying, "You didn't think that with six kids, we'd know how to have an only child, did you?"  That said it all.  I asked my mom later why they had given me such a great day, and she told me, they thought I needed it. With three children already through College , they knew from experience how exhausting Senior year was, and they thought I could use the attention. Further, knowing I was about to graduate and would be interviewing, they knew that I didn't have a lot of professional clothes, so I had a physical need for a blazer. They nailed both needs with one gift.

The gift doesn't have to be physical, either. Sometimes attention, time, and listening are the greatest gifts you can give or get.

Why did the rulers of far-off countries gift Jesus in Matthew? Respect. A gift can show respect to the receiver. Or gratitude. The concept of hostess gifts has pretty much gone by the wayside, but there are still a handful of us who bring a hostess gift to dinner parties as a way of thanking the hostess for her generosity. What about just kindness? The gift can say more about the giver than the receiver. You found something that made you think of someone, and you made/purchased/got it for the other person. It's just a kindness.

So, how do we receive gifts? Well, speaking from experience, I often do it with a red face and comments of, "No, you shouldn't have," or some joke about it not being a holiday or birthday. How rude! What am I thinking? I know, see above—embarrassment, fear of reciprocity, etc.

So, for years now I've been working on my acceptance of gifts. I even have a list of things I tell people to do when I give gifts, if they start my litany of reasons why they shouldn't. First, say thank you—it shows respect to your mother, who taught you to say thank you; it shows appreciation to the giver. You want to do that, don't you? Third, it's polite. Even if somebody is simply handing you something you dropped on the street, you thank them, right? So why would we do less with a gift somebody took time to bring us?

Physically, you take it. You don't leave somebody holding a gift out to you and just look at them. When you refuse a gift, it can hurt a person's feelings. Here's my theory: they wouldn't have given it to you if they didn't want you to have it. Have you had a gift returned or rejected? It's not a great feeling, especially if you were excited about giving it. So, verbally accept the gift, and physically take the gift. There! It's done. That wasn't so hard, was it?

There's a bit more here. When we accept a gift, we should do so gently. Have you ever had a compliment rejected? You tell someone they look nice and the response is, "I'm a mess," or "this old dress?" That doesn't make you feel great, and you were doing something nice. So if you snatch the gift and throw it on a chair, it disrespects the gift and the giver. We could suggest that the gift be accepted graciously, but I think gently is a better description.

But where's the Scriptural lesson in this? Well, of all the gifts in the world, there's only one gift that allows us into heaven. For all the things we accumulate in this world, and all the gifts of compliments we may receive while we're here; and whether we accept gifts graciously or rudely, there's one gift that we can't take a chance on refusing.

The Lord sent His son. Yep, Jesus was in heaven with His Father and the Holy Spirit, from the very beginning. The fact is that in Genesis 1:1 – "In the beginning, God created the heavens and the earth" – a plural is used for the word God, confirming that the trinity was always in existence. But God sent Jesus out of heaven, to a sinful and depraved world, so we would have a path, a bridge, to heaven.

In John 14:6, Jesus Himself says, "I am the truth, the way, and the life. Nobody comes to the Father but through Me." There it is. The only way to heaven, is through Christ. Christ is a gift, available to all.

Some people choose to look at the gift, and reject it. They see the gift, they hear about the gift, but they choose their lifestyle over this glowing gift. Others see it, and even want it, but decide to open it at some other time. It's for these people that we ask the question, "What if you're hit by a truck on the way home tonight?" Nobody knows the time of their death, so sooner is better when accepting the gift of eternal life.

Some people see the gift, want the gift, but are afraid to accept it. The fear may come because it would offend their family, or they fear they'll be laughed at by friends. I could have so easily been one of these! Being raised in a conservative household, I had always attended Church. But, through 20 years of living this way, it wasn't until I was a Junior in College that I finally heard and understood the need for a personal acceptance of Jesus Christ as my Savior. So I did that, but I didn't share the information with my family.

After some maturity and growth, I chose to start worshiping in a Church other than the one in which I had been raised. Oh, my, did that cause a tempest! Praise the Lord I was strong enough in the Lord by that time to make my decision. In fact, Scripture confirmed my decision, because in Matthew 10, we see that "brother will betray brother to death, and a father his child; children will rebel against their parents and have them put to death. All men will hate you because of Me, but he who stands firm to the end will be saved" (vv 21-22).

I'm not saying that I had my brother put to death, but while leaving that Church may have seemed rebellious, it was the right decision for me. If I had chosen to not offend my family, I may not have received blessings the Lord had for me.

I see people who see the truth, want to have a personal relationship with Christ, but are afraid to accept it. Now's the time! You're not turning your back on your family or your friends when you turn to Christ. You may be the first in a long line of followers.

Again, choose today whom you should serve, "as for me and my house, we will serve the Lord" (Joshua 24:15). You are being offered the most precious gift in the world, dear Saints. Don't allow embarrassment, fear, or any other reason keep you from reaching out, accepting the gift, and saying a gentle, "thank you." (February 2010)